JONAH

RELUCTANT PROPHET, MERCIFUL GOD

TAYLOR SANDLIN

Annual Bible Study

Teaching Guide

SMYTH&HELWYS
PUBLISHING INCORPORATED · MACON, GEORGIA

Smyth & Helwys Publishing, Inc.
6316 Peake Road
Macon, Georgia 31210-3960
1-800-747-3016

Library of Congress Catalog-in-Publication Data

Names: Sandlin, Taylor, author.
Title: Jonah : reluctant prophet, merciful God / by Taylor Sandlin.
Description: Macon : Smyth & Helwys, 2016. | Series: Annual Bible
study
Identifiers: LCCN 2016040790 | ISBN 9781573129107 (pbk. : alk.
paper)
Subjects: LCSH: Bible. Jonah--Homiletical use.
Classification: LCC BS1605.55 .S26 2016 | DDC 224/.9207--dc23
LC record available at https://lccn.loc.gov/2016040790

CONTENTS

Annual Bible Study

P. Keith Gammons
Publisher / Executive Vice
President

Leslie Andres
Editor

Kelley F. Land
Assistant Editor

Katie Brookins
Associate Editor

**Daniel Emerson
Dave Jones
Michelle Meredith**
Graphic Design

All Scripture references come from
the NRSV unless otherwise noted.

Most sidebar material has been
adapted from James D. Nogalski,
The Book of the Twelve: Hosea–Jonah,
Smyth & Helwys Bible Commentary
(Macon GA: Smyth & Helwys, 2011).

1-800-747-3016 (USA)

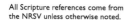
SMYTH&HELWYS
PUBLISHING INCORPORATED   MACON GEORGIA

WWW.HELWYS.COM

Dedicated to my parents,
who first taught me the stories of our faith.

ACKNOWLEDGMENTS

Many people helped me bring this work to completion. I owe each my thanks. I am grateful to Smyth & Helwys Publishing for the opportunity to study and write about the book of Jonah. Keith Gammons did much to help this pastor take steps toward becoming a writer. Leslie Andres offered many helpful suggestions that made my writing appear better than it is. Their patience with me during this process served as a living example of the God who is slow to anger and abounding in love. Becky Ethington and Christi Christian, my assistants, served as proofreaders and helped me clarify my often muddled thoughts. I am especially grateful for the saints who worship at Southland Baptist Church for allowing me the time to study and write. Their participation in the gospel fills me with joy on a daily basis. Above all, I am grateful to my wife, Alyson, and two children, Sophie and John Curtis, for tolerating all the times I was swallowed by my office to meditate and write about the reluctant prophet who was swallowed by that great big fish.

PREFACE

The story of Jonah is one of the most enduring stories in the Bible. Even people who have never read the Bible, much less any of the Minor Prophets, have heard the story of Jonah and the whale. Jonah's popularity has remained strong for good reasons. It is an excellent story filled with humor, irony, suspense, and salvation by unconventional means. Jonah's story is simple enough to entertain children but deep enough to challenge the faith of the eldest saints. It makes sense not only that this story endures but also that God's people continue to champion its retelling time and time again.

When we reread Jonah, we discover that the story in our children's books and the story in our adult memories may not precisely match the one in the biblical text. First, the Bible makes no mention of a whale. Instead, it speaks of a great fish that plays only a minor role in the story. The true protagonist of the story is not the fish. It is not even Jonah. Instead, God is the main character. God calls Jonah. God sends the storm. God provides the fish. God forgives the Ninevites. God questions Jonah. If anything, this story that we know as "Jonah and the Whale" would be more appropriately titled "God and the Prophet Jonah."

Second, while we often remember the story as a quaint narrative with a simple moral, a rereading of the story reveals a far more complex book. The story of Jonah is not a simple morality tale like that of Pinocchio. Instead, the book of Jonah is a story that wrestles with difficult questions about the nature of God. What kind of God is the God of Israel? Who falls within the sphere of God's care? Do some sins demand punishment? Does God's kindness toward evildoers mean that God is unjust?

Far from wrapping everything up with a nice moral lesson, the story of Jonah leaves the reader hanging without providing a simple resolution. The reader is left to ponder, "How will I respond when God loves the people I love to hate?" This question is as relevant today as it has ever been. Conflicts abound in our world between all manner of people. Oppression and violence continue to exist and often triumph in many parts of the world. Christians rightly stand up to oppression and violence wherever we see it, but what does Jonah say to us about our concern for the oppressors? Should we care about the well-being of those who oppress others? If so, what shape should that concern take? How might it conflict with our care for the victims of oppression? Answers are not easy to discover. Perhaps that is why it is time for a rereading of this ancient story of God, the prophet Jonah, and yes, that great, big fish!

INTRODUCTION:
A WHALE OF A TALE

Intro for Ad

The book of Jonah is short. Its four chapters contain only fifty-eight verses. Individual psalms have more verses than this brief book. Despite its brevity, or maybe because of it, Jonah stands out as one of the most recognized stories in the Bible. It is by far the most popular among the twelve books of the Minor Prophets. While the average churchgoer might be pressed to name a majority of those books, even some people who do not attend church regularly have heard the story of Jonah and the big fish. The reason is simple enough: the book of Jonah is a captivating story.

Other books in the Minor Prophets contain narrative elements, but they are primarily collections of prophetic sayings. As such, they are more akin to sermons than stories. While sermons can be powerful forms of communication in the moment, they do not always translate well over time. Modern people, far removed from the time and context of those ancient prophets, struggle to discern the meaning in ancient texts. Sermons are time-bound. Stories, on the other hand, have a way of transcending the generations. Disney has proven that even the oldest stories can still captivate modern audiences. Beauty and the Beast, Sleeping Beauty, and Cinderella were popular fairy tales hundreds of years before they took shape as modern animated movies. A good story has staying power. This explains part of Jonah's continuing appeal. Unlike the other books of the Minor Prophets, Jonah contains only a single sentence of prophetic utterance. In Hebrew, this sermon is just five words long. The majority of the book is a narrative, inviting modern readers into an ancient tale.

The outlandish nature of this story can cause some people to dismiss the tale as being nothing more than the biblical version of Pinocchio. While it is true that children love the story of Jonah, it would be a mistake to assume that this story is only for or even primarily for children. Stories, even fanciful ones,

Jonah in Jewish Tradition

Not surprisingly, the legendary material surrounding Jonah in rabbinic sources is more extensive than that of most of the other prophets in the Book of the Twelve. Traditions grew about this prophet concerning his background, his time on the ship, his time in the fish, and the aftermath of his preaching to the Ninevites. Rabbinic tradition claims Jonah was a disciple of Elisha and anointed Jehu king of Israel. One of the reasons Jonah was concerned about YHWH's proclivity toward forgiveness was that Jonah was already known as a false prophet because he predicted the fall of Jerusalem. However, after its people repented, YHWH relented about destroying Jerusalem. This change, however, reflected negatively on Jonah's veracity, and Israelites began to see Jonah as a false prophet. Jonah's concern about YHWH showing compassion in 4:2 was thus interpreted to have less to do with Jonah's dislike of foreigners than with protecting his reputation as a reliable prophet.

The people on board the ship, according to rabbinic legend, came from the 70 nations of the world. The people on the ship did not want to kill Jonah so they tested the effect by dunking Jonah three times. The first time they dunked him into the water up to his knees, and the sea calmed until they took him out. Then they placed him into the sea up to his neck (cf. 2:5 [MT 2:6]) and again the sea got calm. Finally, they were convinced that they had to throw him in if they wanted to survive. Subsequently, the conversion of the pagan sailors is recounted even more dramatically by the rabbis than by the book of Jonah.

Several traditions, both competing and harmonizing, can be detected in rabbinic material about Jonah's time in the fish. One tradition arises from the use of two different words for fish in the narrative, twice masculine (1:17 and 2:10) and once feminine (2:1). The harmonizing traditions thus put Jonah in a masculine fish first.

This fish was appointed from the beginning of time to be ready for Jonah. However, this fish was also destined to be destroyed by Leviathan once Jonah was inside. Jonah, however, convinced Leviathan not to eat the fish. Out of gratitude the male fish gives Jonah the ride of his life, showing him the great undersea marvels of the world. As a result, Jonah is having such a great time that God sends a female fish that is pregnant with 365,000 baby fish to take Jonah. At that point, Jonah's discomfort forces him to pray for deliverance. The heat from the belly of the fish dissolves his garments, makes his hair fall out, and causes sores to develop on his body. These ailments add to his discomfort when waiting in the sun outside Nineveh.

In rabbinic tradition, Jonah learns a valuable lesson from YHWH's speech to him after YHWH destroys the plant. Jonah shows contrition. He prostrates himself and implores YHWH: "O God, guide the world according to your goodness." Thus, while the book of Jonah ends with an open-ended question, rabbinic tradition tends to portray Jonah as having been enlightened by the experience with the plant and the worm. Jonah's punishment in the fish had been so severe that Jonah was spared death and taken to paradise while he was yet living. Nineveh's deliverance lasted as long as their repentance. At the end of the 40 days, they returned to their sinful ways and Jonah's prophecy overtook them. This last portion ties specifically into Nahum (see Beatte Ego, "The Repentance of Nineveh in the Story of Jonah and Nahum's Prophecy of the City's Destruction: Aggadic Solutions for an Exegetical Problem in the Book of the Twelve," in Aaron Schart and Paul Redditt, eds., *Thematic Threads in the Book of the Twelve* [Beihefte zur Zeitschrift für die alttestamentliche Wissenschaft 325; Berlin De Gruyter, 2003] 155–64).

For additional reading, see Louis Ginzberg, *The Legends of the Jews*, 7 vols. (Philadelphia: The Jewish Publication Society of America, 1947) 4:246–53 and 6:343–52.

are the principal way humans make sense of the world. Even the non-narrative portions of the Bible find their truest meaning when they are understood in the context of the overarching narrative of the Scriptures. While a person can make some sense out of the Ten Commandments as a stand-alone text, these commandments come alive when placed in the context of the larger narrative about Israel's deliverance from Egypt and the nation's election as God's people. Understanding the Bible as story allows us to connect our individual stories with the story of God. Eugene Peterson puts it well: "The biblical story invites us in as participants in something larger than our sin-defined needs, into something truer than our culture stunted ambitions. We enter these stories and recognize ourselves as participants, whether willing or unwilling, in the life of God."[1] Few stories invite us to experience an enlarging of our world quite like the story of Jonah. We may find ourselves interested in the story about Jonah and the big fish, but what we soon discover is that this is actually a story about God and us.

GENRE

What kind of story is Jonah? Scholars disagree about the actual genre of this book even as they agree on its narrative format. The book of Jonah has been classified as a novella, satire, comedy, parable, and even Midrash. Midrash is a specific kind of Jewish literature that serves as a commentary on biblical texts. Jonah has some affinities with Midrashic literature. The story does offer a contrasting or illuminating word to other texts in the Bible. Unfortunately, scholars cannot agree about which text Jonah is specifically addressing. Nahum, Amos, Joel 2:13-14, and Jeremiah 18:7-10 have all been proposed. As we shall see, Jonah presents the reader with an alternate voice among the Minor Prophets. Nevertheless, it is probably

The Genre of Jonah

A *novella* is a short novel. Those who see Jonah as a *satire* see the focus of the message as poking fun at the narrow-minded theological perspective Jonah represents. A *midrash* is a genre unique to Judaism. It is a story told to explain a theological point that is generally related to a biblical text. In the case of Jonah, it has often been suggested that Jonah is a midrash on Jer 18:7-10, a text that articulates YHWH's freedom to act in judgment or salvation toward any nation.

shortsighted to limit the book's role to that of commentary. Jonah has its own story to tell and should be allowed to stand on its own two feet.

While narrowing down the genre of the story can help us with our interpretation of the book, Jonah resists such characterization. Still, a few things can be noted about this tale. First, the book is filled with irony. The storyteller constantly turns the reader's expectations upside down. God's prophet proves disobedient. Pagans prove insightful. What is expected almost never occurs. Second, the story is purposefully sensational. Big storms and big fish help grab and keep the reader's attention. Third, the story is didactic. That is, it is a story that aims to teach. All of the ironic and sensational elements entertain the reader, but they also help the reader become aware of truths that reside just beyond one's expectations. Jonah teaches us truths about God. It also teaches us truths about ourselves as the people of God.

FACT OR FICTION?

For many people, one question quickly rises to the surface when studying the book of Jonah: "Is it true?" What they usually mean by this question is, "Did this really happen? Did a man named Jonah actually get swallowed by a fish and live in its belly for three days?" Those who are unfamiliar with the church might not realize the challenges this question poses for the average Bible study teacher. While some scholars dismiss the historicity of the story without even discussing the issue, many laypeople assume the story actually happened and are stunned when someone suggests otherwise. How should a teacher navigate this issue with her class? Obviously, one's context matters. In certain settings, questions about the historicity of this book will barely raise an eyebrow. In other settings, the same question will set the entire class on edge. This is especially true when issues of historicity become a litmus test to determine orthodoxy on the one hand or intelligence on the other. In such discussions, Jonah becomes a battleground for larger ecclesial and cultural struggles. Those who believe the story of Jonah is fiction, akin to one of the parables of Jesus, can be tempted to judge those who believe the story actually happened to be lacking in sophistication. Those who hold to the historicity of this story can be tempted to accuse those who do not of failing to believe in miracles, thus undermining the authority of the Scriptures. Neither form of judgment is helpful in the interpretation of the book. It does not do much for the spirit of the church, either. How one answers the question, "Did this actually happen?" does not prove either orthodoxy or intelligence. Orthodox, intelligent people answer this question in a variety of ways. How one answers the question of historicity does little to determine whether or not one hears the message of this book. In fact, spending too much time on issues of historicity can cause a class to miss the deeper truths that Jonah intends to convey.

Despite the potential pitfalls, I do not think it is helpful to dodge the question of historicity altogether. At least a few students will have questions of this nature. Dodging the question can make it look as if the teacher has either not done her homework or, worse, has something to hide. For this reason, it is best to address this aquatic elephant in the room early on. Another reason for addressing the issue involves the missional potential of the book. For some skeptics of the Christian faith, the uncritical acceptance of the Jonah story as historical fact by some Christians keeps them from interacting with the text. These skeptics want no part of an anti-intellectual faith. I have found that admitting the story might not have literally happened invites skeptics to engage the story on the story's own terms. If we can get skeptics to engage the story of Jonah seriously, they will likely discover there a portrait of God that is both richer and fuller than the one they expected to find. Ultimately, our goal is not to convince people one way or the other about the historicity of this book. Instead, our goal is to introduce people to the very real God who can be met in its pages. It is worth entertaining the question, "Did this really happen?" if it helps get us to the better questions: "What is God like?" and "What does God desire for our lives?"

While a full consideration of the historicity of the story might pave the way for a hearing among skeptics, the same discussion can cause all manner of trouble in more traditional church settings. I have found two things helpful when discussing the historicity of the book of Jonah in congregations that might be leery of any suggestion that something in the Bible did not happen as it is printed on the page. First, it is helpful to reassert what we believe about God. Any God who can raise Jesus from the dead is capable of keeping a person alive in the belly of a fish. Christians who believe in miracles, especially the miracle of the resurrection, at least hold out the possibility that this miracle might have occurred. That being said, it is also important to ask, "Does the historicity of the Jonah story make a difference in the meanings we draw from it?" I do not think it does. A story can convey truth, even deep truths, without being historical. The majority of the stories Jesus told were fictional stories that conveyed spiritual truths. Take Jesus' story about the man with two sons in Luke 15:11-32, for example. It is clear from the way Jesus tells the story that he means for us to understand this parable as a fictional tale. Nevertheless, few stories convey as much truth as the story of the prodigal sons and their loving father. The same could be said about the story of Jonah. Could it have happened? Yes. Does the truth this book conveys depend on its historicity? No. Remember, the big fish is a minor character in this story. Spending too much time on the fish causes us to miss the larger, more important truths about God's mercy toward sinners.

That being said, it can be helpful for a class to understand the basic arguments for and against historicity. Scholars who argue for a literal reading of this story usually point to the fact that Jonah is a historical figure in the Old Testament (see 2 Kings 14:25). These scholars indicate that the introduction of the book not only connects this story to that historical character but also mirrors other historical sections of the Scriptures, including the stories of Elijah and Elisha. They view this as an implicit sign that the author intends for us to view the story as if it actually happened.[2] Many proponents of a more literal reading also point out that Christian and Jewish teachers have traditionally viewed the book as historical. For instance, Josephus includes the story of Jonah and the big fish in his history of the Jewish people (*Antiquities* 9.206-214). These scholars maintain that tradition should not be discarded too quickly for modern assumptions about what is possible in the material world. Most scholars who continue to believe in the basic historicity of the book acknowledge that the historical veracity of the book cannot be proven, but they argue that it should not be dismissed out of hand.[3]

Scholars who argue against the historicity of the book acknowledge that the author of Jonah has connected his account to a historical figure from 2 Kings but also maintain that this is a rhetorical device and not an indication of historicity. Scholars who doubt the historicity generally maintain that the exaggerated language of the text points to an artfully crafted story of fiction, not a historical retelling of an actual event. The improbable swallowing of Jonah by the fish and the mass conversion of the Ninevites, which appears nowhere else outside the biblical text, drive the plot in the same way that far-fetched details drive the plot in some of Jesus' parables. For instance, when Jesus speaks about a king who forgave the debt of a man who owed ten thousand talents, the listener knows this is an absurd amount of money (Matt 18:23-35). The point of the parable is driven home by the absurdly large amount of money that the king forgave. In much the same way, the outlandish nature of the story of Jonah serves a profound literary point. God's grace upends our expectations. While it could be true that an author has retold a historical narrative in an artful way, the exaggerations and ironic twists of the story point toward a didactic aim more than a journalistic one (that is, aiming to offer a moral rather than convey a true account). It is this didactic aim that should most concern the reader.[4] Here both groups of scholars agree that the point of the story resides well beyond questions of historicity.

DATE OF COMPOSITION

The only consensus concerning the dating of the composition of Jonah is that there is no consensus. The earliest Jonah could have been composed is the middle of the eighth century BCE during Jeroboam II's reign (786–746 BCE). The latest it could be dated is the third century BCE when the book of Jonah gets mentioned in Tobit, a deuterocanonical text composed at that time. Attempts to place the composition of Jonah more specifically within that range have proved fruitless, with many scholars conceding that "the actual composition of the book is not datable except within the broadest of boundaries."[5]

Some scholars do attempt to place the concerns of this book into a more specific time frame. Fretheim, for instance, argues that the author of Jonah uses the prophet as a "vehicle for describing his own contemporaries. That is, Jonah's thoughts and actions are sketched by the author in such a way as to parallel those of the audience to which the book is addressed."[6] That is likely true. The difficulty remains in determining just who the author's original audience was. Some see the message of Jonah as a corrective to the harsh nationalism of Ezra and Nehemiah. Fretheim argues for the earlier period of the prophet Malachi (475–450 BCE). Malachi does ask questions about whether or not a life of following God proves worth all the effort. During the time of Malachi, Jews had impoverished lives that failed to live up to the promises of the prophets (Isa 40–66; Joel 3). Meanwhile, it seemed as if pagan powers prospered despite their clear sins. Malachi laments, "All who do evil are good in the sight of the

LORD, and he delights in them" (Mal 2:17). Fretheim argues that the character of Jonah represents Jews who are fed up with the perceived injustice of God's actions toward Jews and pagan powers alike.[7] Fretheim is an excellent writer and he makes his case well; nevertheless, his hypothesis remains well in the area of conjecture. There simply is no one explanation as to when Jonah was written.

SETTING

It is much easier to determine the literary setting of the book than to date it. The author of Jonah clearly connects the main character, Jonah the son of Amittai (1:1), with the prophet named in 2 Kings 14:25. In Kings, the reader learns that Jonah was a prophet born in the town of Gath-Hepher. He prophesied in the northern kingdom during the reign of Jeroboam II (786–746 BCE). Jeroboam was an evil king, but Jonah brought a good word to him from the Lord that Israel's borders would be restored to its previous grandeur. God did this not because of anything Jeroboam had done but instead because God had pity on the desperate state of the people of Israel (2 Kings 14:26-27). The book of Jonah, then, is set in the same period but moves from the kingdom of Israel to the kingdom of Assyria.

The question of Assyria weighed heavily upon eighth-century Israel. In the previous century, Assyria had risen to prominence under the leadership of two powerful leaders, Ashurnasirpal II (883–859 BCE) and Shalmaneser III (859–824 BCE). For a short while, Israel held its own against its larger neighbor. King Omri and King Ahab drew the ire of Jewish prophets, but they succeeded in making alliances with Assyria that led to the expansion of Israel's borders and to significant building projects within the kingdom.[8] This expansion came at a high cost. As Assyria grew stronger, Israel degenerated from being a rival in the region to being a vassal state. During the early seventh century BCE, Assyria experienced a period of decline. In this time of weakness, Assyria waged fewer wars against its neighbors, dealt with domestic rebellions, and suffered a severe famine in its land. This decline opened the door for Jeroboam II, and Israel gained back much of its lost territory. These gains would be short lived, however. The rise of Tiglath-pileser III (745–727 BCE) led to an Assyrian resurgence. Tiglath-pileser III's successors, Shalmaneser V (727–722 BCE) and Sargon II (722–705 BCE), destroyed Israel's capital, Samaria, and brought the

Kings of Assyria

 The eighth-century kings of Assyria are well known because of the extensive records they kept.

Assyrian Kings	Notes
Adad-nirari III (811–783 BCE)	
Shalmaneser IV (783–773 BCE)	Jeroboam II (king of Israel 786–746 BCE)
Ashur-Dan III (773–755 BCE)	
Ashur-nirari V (755–745 BCE)	
Tiglath-Pileser III (745–727 BCE)	
Shalmaneser V (727–722 BCE)	Destruction of Samaria (722 BCE)
Sargon II (722–705 BCE; co-regency with Shalmaneser V from 722–709 BCE)	
Sennacherib (705–681 BCE)	c. 700 Sennacherib moves capital to Nineveh

Assyria had four different kings during the reign of Jeroboam II, the king when Jonah was prophet (according to 2 Kgs 14:25). Nineveh was not the capital of Assyria until the time of Sennacherib. During the eighth century, especially beginning with Tiglath-Pileser III, Assyria expanded westward toward the Mediterranean. By the middle of the seventh century, it had conquered territory all the way to Egypt (see discussion in Nah 3:8).

---

northern kingdom to an end in 722 BCE.[9] According to Syrian records, 27,000 Israelites were deported and cities across the country were destroyed.[10]

The Assyrians did not just capture their enemies. They terrorized them, and then they boasted about their reign of terror. Archaeologists have uncovered large carvings in Assyrian palaces that reveal gruesome battle scenes as well as written accounts of post-battle torture of prisoners that rival the worst violence Hollywood has ever thought up. As James Bruckner notes,

> Records brag of live dismemberment, often leaving one hand attached so they could shake it before the person died. They made parades of heads, requiring friends of the deceased to carry them elevated on poles. They boasted of their practice of stretching live prisoners with ropes so they could be skinned alive. The human skins were then displayed on city walls and on poles. . . . They pulled out the tongues and testicles of live victims and burned the young alive.[11]

Assyrian dominance and the terror that accompanied it would last until 612 BCE when Nineveh fell to the combined armies of the Medes and Babylonians.

It is not surprising that the book of Nahum celebrates the fall of Nineveh. The prophet declares that it is a "city of bloodshed, utterly deceitful," with "flashing sword and glittering spear, piles of dead, heaps of corpses, dead bodies without end" (Nah 3:1, 3). All who hear of its demise "clap their hands over you. For who has ever escaped your endless cruelty?" (Nah 3:19). More surprising is the book of Jonah's more favorable picture of this terrible city. In the book of Jonah, the Ninevites are considered evildoers. Their wickedness is what stirs God's action in the first place (1:2). Jonah is called to preach *against* the city. What is remarkable is that the Ninevites respond to Jonah's preaching. When the king of Nineveh repents, he orders all of his people to "turn from their evil ways and from the violence that is in their hands" (3:8b), and the people comply (3:10). The Lord then relents from destroying Nineveh. This leaves Jonah furious. In his mind, people like the Ninevites deserve to be punished, not spared. To Jonah, forgiveness, in this instance, makes a mockery of justice. God challenges Jonah's anger, asking, "Should I not be concerned about Nineveh?" (4:11a). Understanding Israel's rocky relationship with Assyria helps the reader grasp Jonah's difficulty in answering that question.

TEACHING JONAH

A class best engages the text of Jonah not by studying its possible composition date but by becoming immersed in the text. Historical questions aside, it is clear that the author has gone to great lengths to tell this story in a literary fashion. Paying attention to the literary nature helps the reader engage the story on its own terms. The story breaks down into four clear scenes: God calls and Jonah flees (1:1-16), God saves and Jonah prays (1:17–2:10), Jonah preaches and the Ninevites repent (3:1-10), Jonah complains and God responds (4:1-11). The book of Jonah starts in Jerusalem, quickly moves to Joppa, takes a detour over the Mediterranean Sea, and ends in Nineveh, a great city in Assyria.

The Hebrew text of Jonah is simple but well composed. The author frequently uses the repetition of words to highlight themes and to connect one portion of the text to another. For instance, God calls Jonah to arise and go up to Nineveh. Instead, Jonah goes down to Joppa, down into the ship, and eventually down into the depths of the sea. God *hurls* a big wind onto the sea, the sailors *hurl* cargo into the sea, and eventually they *hurl* Jonah there as well. This technique would have been especially useful in an oral culture, helping both storytellers and hearers to remember the story. Sometimes English translations, like the NRSV, lose a bit of this repetition, choosing to translate a single word in Hebrew with several different English words. This may help the text read more smoothly in English, but it causes the English reader to miss some of the author's skill in using repetition. Other translations, like the NASB and the CEB, do a better job of rendering the repetition in English.

The repetition of two words proves especially meaningful. The first is the adjective "great," sometimes translated "important." This word appears fourteen times in Jonah: great city (1:2), great wind, great storm (1:4), great fear (1:10), great storm (1:12), great fear (1:16), great fish (1:17), great city (3:2), great city (3:3), from the greatest (3:5), great ones (3:7), great anger (4:1), great gladness (4:6), great city (4:11). The repeated use of the word "great" contrasts Jonah's level of concern for the people of Nineveh. While Jonah shows great concern over a little plant, he shows almost no concern for the great city of Nineveh. God, on the other hand, shows great concern for great big cities and for petulant little prophets.

The second word that plays a major role in the text is "evil." The word can mean either *wickedness* or *troubles*, and it takes both forms in this text. In both 3:8 and 3:10, the word clearly means *evil*. The Ninevites have committed evil and repent of it. In six other occurrences (1:7, 8; 3:10; 4:1, 2, and 6), it carries the connotation of *trouble* or *calamity*. The sailors cast lots to determine who has brought this calamity upon them. The most ambiguous occurrence is the first in 1:2. The reader is left to wonder, is it the wickedness of the Ninevites that has stirred God to action or the calamity of judgment that is about to fall upon them that moves God to speak? Clearly, the two evils are tied together. The Ninevites' evil ways have led them to the precipice of destruction. Nevertheless, God's anger at their sin is coupled with a genuine concern for their plight. Yes, they have brought this upon themselves, but God has compassion even on those who bring trouble upon their own heads.

The repetition of words and the use of irony do more than entertain; they help drive the main themes of the text. The narrative nature of Jonah means the theme or point of the story is not explicit. As a result, interpreters of the book have highlighted a variety of theological themes over the years. Most of these themes center on God's activity. God is referenced thirty-nine times in fifty-eight verses. In those thirty-nine times, God's sovereignty is on clear display. God drives almost all of the action. God calls Jonah. While God permits Jonah the freedom to respond in the negative, God remains committed to helping

Jonah obey. God does this primarily by exerting control over nature. God sends the wind. God sends the fish. God provides the plant. God sends the worm. Beyond the natural world, God's sovereignty extends over God's own previous statements. While God calls Jonah to deliver a word of judgment over Nineveh, God remains free to alter course. As James Nogalski puts it, the God we find in the book of Jonah is a God who is "in complete control, who can act unilaterally, and who can reverse course when deemed appropriate."[12]

Some interpreters of the book focus on God's call of Jonah. Throughout the Scriptures, God calls prophets to deliver a word to God's people. Unlike other instances of prophetic calling in the Scriptures, God calls Jonah to go not to God's people but to a foreign people. While other prophets showed initial reluctance to the call of God on their lives, Jonah's is the only example we have of someone who actively flees the call of God. Nevertheless, God's call on Jonah's life remains strong throughout the text. Jonah's place in the canon reminds the reader that God does not call robots to join in the divine work, but fallible, stubborn, sinful people. It should not be surprising that people struggle with the call of God on their lives. Eugene Peterson picks up this theme in his delightful work *Under the Unpredictable Plant: An Exploration in Vocational Holiness*, arguing, "The Jonah story is sharply evocative of the vocation experience of the pastor."[13] Peterson's work is more of an allegorical application of the text to the pastor's life than it is a commentary on the text. Nevertheless, it reveals how the story of Jonah and God still connects to our own stories with God today. Since Jonah is never specifically called a prophet in this book, we should resist the urge to think that Jonah's story of calling only applies to those in vocational ministry. God calls us all.

Closely related to the theme of calling is the theme of God's heart for the nations. As far back as Augustine, interpreters of the book have seen Jonah as a text that emphasizes the missionary concern of God. Unfortunately, this line of interpretation has sometimes devolved into anti-Semitic propaganda. Some interpreters have viewed Jonah as a symbol of Jewish enmity toward Gentiles. A close reading of Jonah precludes this line of reasoning. Jonah is not anti-Gentile. In fact, he is willing to sacrifice himself for the welfare of the Gentile sailors. Jonah *is* anti-Ninevite, but this seems to have much more to do with their wickedness than their status as Gentiles. What is clear in the text is that God is not anti-Ninevite or anti-Gentile. God shows concern for the Ninevites, the sailors, and, lest one forget, Jonah, too. The careful interpreter should resist the temptation to see modern missionary concerns in Jonah's mission. He does not go to Nineveh to convert them into Jews. Nor does God seem to expect such a conversion even in the Ninevites' repentance. God threatens to punish the Ninevites because of their wickedness and violence, not their idolatry. Other parts of the Scriptures may give us more clues as to God's ultimate desires for the peoples of the earth to be converted to the worship of the one true God. Jonah hints in that direction, but the missionary concern is not primary. What Jonah does reaffirm, with other passages in the Bible, is that even pagan kingdoms act justly toward others.

Ultimately, the question of God's justice and mercy dominates this short book. As noted above, Jonah does not despise the Ninevites because they are Gentiles. Jonah despises the Assyrians because they are evil. Jonah gets absolutely no argument from God about this fact. The Assyrians were evil. To this day, history remembers not only their brutality toward others but also their delight in that brutality. Jonah flees God's call not because he is fearful of the Ninevites but because he is fearful that God will show them mercy (4:2). On more than one occasion, Jonah appears more than ready to die. What Jonah is not ready for is a world in which evildoers like the Assyrians get off scot-free. For all the modern talk of life without judgment, most people want God to judge evildoers like the Assyrians. We, like Jonah, might vehemently resist delivering a word from God to ISIS soldiers or child molesters if we believed it would lead to their full and complete pardon. While Jonah's argument with God strikes modern readers as completely unrighteous, his prophetic protest of God's own actions does serve a purpose. Throughout the Hebrew Scriptures, God's people struggle and argue with God as a way of discovering the truth. Students who struggle with the text of Jonah engage in the same pursuit.

How can we struggle through the text in a way that leads to a renewed understanding of God's nature and God's calling on our lives? One way is by paying attention to the questions the text asks and learning to ask our own. This short book contains fourteen questions. Most are aimed at Jonah. He is first grilled by the captain (1:6) and then the sailors (1:8, 10, 11). Jonah asks questions of God (2:4, 4:2), and God does not hesitate to ask questions of him (4:4, 9, 11). Even the king of Nineveh gets in on the act (3:9), asking a question that is so theologically rich, it echoes Joel 2:14: "Who knows? God may relent and change his mind."

The book of Jonah gives us permission to question what we have learned about God's view of evildoers. While Ezra and Nehemiah and some of the Proverbs show a genuine concern for the negative influence of outsiders on the people of God, Jonah asks serious questions about whether those passages are the only divine word on the subject. The book of Jonah asks out loud if God might be equally concerned about evildoers' welfare as God is about the influence evildoers have on others. These questions open the door to difficult questions about justice and mercy, sin and repentance. Jonah's protest should not be viewed purely in terms of disobedience. Jonah's discomfort with God's mercy resonates with anyone who has ever desired to see evildoers pay for their sins. The questions aimed at Jonah stir within us the same discomfort that Jesus does when he challenges his followers,

> Love your enemies and pray for those who persecute you, so that you may be children of your Father in heaven; for he makes his sun rise on the evil and on the good, and sends rain on the righteous and on the unrighteous. For if you love those who love you, what reward do you have? Do not even the tax collectors do the same? If you greet only your brothers and sisters, what more are you doing than others? Do not even the Gentiles do the same? (Matt 5:44-47)

It is easy to aim those questions at others. It is more difficult to have them aimed at us. When the question is about our lives and our very real enemies, will we submit to this kind of questioning, or will we, like Jonah, do our best to skip town?

QUESTIONS FOR REFLECTION AND DISCUSSION

1. Jonah is a story that is familiar to many. In what contexts have you encountered this story before? How do these previous encounters with the story shape your interpretation of the text?

2. How does the conversation about Jonah's historical accuracy affect your reading of the story? Can you articulate the reasons some people might hold a view different from your own? What things do you share in common despite your disagreements?

3. Jonah is often presented primarily as a negative example. We are often encouraged, "Don't be like Jonah." What characteristics of Jonah might prove beneficial in our lives?

4. Questions play a big role in the book of Jonah. Jonah questions God and God questions Jonah. What role do questions play in your faith journey?

SUGGESTIONS FOR WORSHIP AND PREACHING

Order of Worship

Prelude

Call to Worship: Psalm 24

"This Is My Father's World"

Welcome and Greeting

"God of Creation, All Powerful" (Margaret Clarkson, 1986, Word Music)

Pastoral Prayer

"Indescribable" (Jesse Reeves and Laura Story, 2004, sixsteps Music)

New Testament Reading: Matthew 13:34-35

"Speak, O Lord" (Keith Getty and Stuart Townend, 2005, Thankyou Music)

Sermon: A Whale of a Tale (Jonah 1:1-3)

Hymn of Commitment: "Wherever He Leads I'll Go" (B. B. McKinney, 1936. Ren. 1964 Broadman Press)

Benediction: Now to him who is able to do far more abundantly than all that we ask or think, according to the power at work within us, to him be glory in the church and in Christ Jesus throughout all generations, forever and ever. Amen. (Eph 3:20-21)

Example Sermon Outline: A Whale of a Tale (Jonah 1:1-3)

The book of Jonah is found in the Bible among the twelve Minor Prophets, which means it can be a little difficult to find. In my Bible, Jonah is just the front and back of a single page. Four short chapters. Fifty-eight verses. Despite its brevity, it is one of the few Minor Prophet books that any of us could name with consistency. More than that, it is one of the few books in this part of the Bible that a majority of churchgoers know anything about. Why is the book of Jonah lodged in our collective memories, while books like Nahum and Habakkuk are not? I think it is because Jonah, unlike the other books in the Minor Prophets, is primarily a story. The other Minor Prophet books have some narrative elements, but they are primarily collections of sayings from the prophets. In a word, they're sermons. Jonah, on the other hand, contains only one short sermon that in Hebrew is just five words long. The rest of the book is story.

People love stories. Stories are memorable. Stories stick with us. Stories transcend the generations. The other books of the Minor Prophets are sermons from a long, long time ago. That makes them especially difficult to understand because sermons tend to speak to specific time. What makes a good sermon in one generation does not necessarily make a good sermon in another. Stories, at least good ones, have a way of remaining popular from one generation to the next. Jonah was written just as long ago as the other prophetic books, but because it is a good story, it stays with us in ways those books do not.

Even though I am a preacher, I know that stories are always more enter-taining than sermons. A good story is almost always better than even the best sermon. We preachers are good at turning good stories into mediocre sermons. We know one of the best ways to help out a bad sermon is to insert a good story into the middle of it. Outside of preachers, most people don't pay to read sermons. People do pay to hear stories for the simple reason that stories are entertaining and engaging.

Few stories are as engaging as the story of Jonah and the big fish. In fact, of all the stories in the Bible, the story of Jonah ranks right up there with Noah's ark and David and Goliath as stories that even non-churchgoers have heard. Like all good stories, the story of Jonah has a great variety of wordplays, plot twists, and repetition of key phrases that help us listen. Remember, this story was probably first told to people who could not read, or who at least did not use the written word as their primary form of communication. As such, Jonah is a story that is meant to be heard as much as it is to be read.

When we listen to the story of Jonah or read it from a translation of Scripture that tries to preserve some of the wordplays, like the NASB and CEB do, we quickly notice that the author of the book of Jonah loves to repeat some key words. The repetition of key words plays an important role in oral communication by helping both storyteller and hearer to remember the story. The first book that either of my children could read, or at least act like they were reading, was the simple book *Brown Bear, Brown Bear*. The truth is, neither of my children could actually read that book at the age of two or three. What they could do was recite it. Why could they recite it? Because it has lots of repetition.

The book of Jonah is not quite that simple, but it does have words that show up again and again. One of those is "big" or "great." There is a great, big city to which God sends Jonah. There is the great, big storm that threatens Jonah and the sailors. There is the great, big fish that swallows Jonah whole. It's the one that helps Jonah get back to the great, big city to tell them the good news God has for the people there. There is also the fact that God provides or appoints things from nature to drive the story along. God sends the fish. God sends a plant. God sends a worm to eat the plant. God sends a wind. One of my favorite wordplays uses the word "hurl." Isn't that a great word? It means *to throw*, not *to vomit*, but that word is in there, too! The Lord hurls a wind on the sea. The sailors are afraid so they hurl the cargo into the sea. Eventually, they hurl Jonah into the sea.

Speaking of Jonah, stories don't just have wordplay; they also have characters. Jonah is a great character because he doesn't do what we expect. Jonah is a prophet of God, which is the Old Testament equivalent of preacher. Prophets are supposed to do what God wants them to do. God wants Jonah to "Arise and go up to Nineveh." Instead, Jonah goes *down*. First he goes down to Joppa, then down into the boat, and then down into the depths of the sea.

In the sea, Jonah gets swallowed by the fish. We think of the fish as a major character, but he's really not. He may be a great, big fish, but he is a minor character in this story, only showing up in a couple of verses. He gets the same airtime as the plant and the worm, but "Jonah and the Fish, Plant, and Worm" isn't quite as catchy a title, is it? There are the sailors and the Ninevites and the king of Nineveh, who are outsiders, but who, like Jonah, flip the script upside down. They understand more about the God of Israel than the prophet of God does.

And then there's God. God is actually the main character of this story. If you read closely, you'll notice that God calls Jonah. God sends the storm. God sends the fish. God saves Jonah from the deep. God instructs the fish to hurl Jonah up on the beach (that part's best with sound effects!). God calls Jonah a second time. God relents when the Ninevites repent of their evil. In chapter 4, God answers Jonah's complaint. God is the protagonist. God acts; others react.

If God is the main character, why is this book not a sermon? Isn't that what prophetic books normally do? Do they not bring us a word from God? Why do we have a story instead of "thus says the Lord"? Perhaps God knows how good we are at ignoring sermons, especially when they say something we don't want to hear. People ask me why I don't preach on giving more often. It's because when I do, giving goes down! When you have something to say to someone that you know they do not want to hear, sermons are not the way to go. People cross their arms and dig in their heels. Stories, on the other hand, have a way of sneaking by our defenses. That's why when the prophet Nathan needed to confront King David about his sin, he used a story. If Nathan had used a sermon, he likely would have lost his prophetic head. That's why he used a story about a man and his little lamb. This is also why Jesus told stories about prodigal sons and good Samaritans to help the pious understand that they still didn't know much about God.

Jonah is one of these kinds of stories: a story that's supposed to sneak past our defenses. We have other sermons in the Minor Prophets—eleven sermons, to be exact. And we have this one story that perhaps longs to teach us something the sermons can't. That leaves us wondering what truth Jonah is attempting to sneak past our defenses. Whose defenses does God want this story to sneak past? Jonah is set in the eighth century BCE. We know this by connecting the Jonah in this book to the Jonah found in 2 Kings 14:25 who prophesied during the reign of Jeroboam II. Assyria, of which Nineveh was a part, had been big and bad prior to Jeroboam's reign and would be big and bad after it. During his reign, they weren't quite as big, but they were just as bad. When I say bad, I mean really bad. Think Hitler bad. ISIS bad. They were bad.

That's the setting of the book, but it may not be the exact setting of the composition of the book. The story may have been told shortly after Jonah's time, or it might have been written to a people much later. Just when Jonah was written is difficult to pin down. We know it was written down before 200 BCE, because another writer mentions it then. But that's about all we know, which puts the range of possibility anytime from 700 BCE–200 BCE. In that time, the people of Israel had been pushed around by any number of big, bad guys: the Assyrians, the Babylonians, the Medes, the Egyptians, and eventually the Romans. The Israelites knew what it meant to suffer under the oppression of foreign powers.

The Israelites knew from their Scriptures, from prophetic sermons, what God was going to do to all these foreign powers. Eventually, God was going to get them. If you read the book of Nahum, you realize it is a book that also addresses the Assyrian empire. In that book, the message is clear: God is going to destroy the Assyrians. In quite colorful language, the prophet celebrates the day when the Ninevites will get what they deserve. Sometimes we need sermons like that. Sermons that assure us that the scales of justice will not always remain unbalanced. Sermons that remind us that one day God will indeed set all things right.

The thing about sermons is that we can sometimes take part of a sermon, a truthful part, and apply it so narrowly that it becomes, in the end, untruth. By taking one sermon as the last word on God's work in the world, we can miss the broader movements of God's Spirit among us. Isn't that what happened to the Pharisees? The Pharisees knew the Bible. They knew the sermons that God's prophets had brought. They interpreted those sermons so narrowly that they missed the broader picture of God's activity in the world. That's why Jesus told them stories about good Samaritans and prodigal sons so that they might see beyond the sermons to the greater story of God's love.

That same God gives us the story of Jonah because it also delivers a message that is tough to hear. Yes, God is going to do something about evil in the world, but that does not mean that God is always against evildoers. God loves the evildoers just as God loves us. Jonah asks a profound question: What will we do when we discover that God loves the people we love to hate? What will God do with us when we object to God's kind of love?

NOTES

1. Eugene Peterson, *Eat this Book* (Grand Rapids MI: Eerdmans, 2006) 41.

2. T. Desmond Alexander, "Jonah: An Introduction and Commentary," in vol. 26 of *Tyndale Old Testament Commentaries* (Downers Grove IL: IVP Academic, 1988) 82.

3. For a full treatment of the arguments in favor of historicity, see Douglas Stuart, *Hosea–Jonah*, Word Biblical Commentary (Grand Rapids MI: Zondervan, 1988) 440–43.

4. For a full treatment of the arguments against historicity, see Terence E. Fretheim, *The Message of Jonah* (Minneapolis: Augsburg, 1977) 61–72.

5. Stuart, *Hosea–Jonah*, 432.

6. Fretheim, *Message of Jonah*, 29.

7. Ibid., 36–37.

8. B. E. Kelle, "Israelite History," *Dictionary of the Old Testament Prophets*, ed. Mark J. Boda and J. Gordon McConville (Downers Grove IL: IVP Academic, 2012) 404–405.

9. James Bruckner, *Jonah, Nahum, Habakkuk, Zephaniah*, The NIV Application Commentary (Grand Rapids MI: Zondervan, 2004) 29.

10. Kelle, "Israelite History," 405.

11. Bruckner, *Jonah, Nahum, Habakkuk, Zephaniah*, 28–29.

12. James D. Nogalski, *The Book of the Twelve: Hosea–Jonah*, Smyth & Helwys Bible Commentary (Macon GA: Smyth & Helwys, 2011) 403.

13. Eugene H. Peterson, *Under the Unpredictable Plant: An Exploration in Vocational Holiness* (Grand Rapids MI: Eerdmans, 1992) 6.

GOD CALLS AND JONAH FLEES

Jonah 1:1-16

Within the first few sentences, the reader knows that the story of Jonah will be nothing like the other prophetic books. The word of the Lord may have come to Jonah as it did to the other prophets, but the similarities stop there. In this instance, the word is not for God's people but for the hated Assyrians. Even more remarkably, Jonah rejects God's assignment. While other prophets resisted God's calling, Jonah is the only one who flees. A violent storm and some terrified sailors keep the action moving in chapter 1, but in the end, Jonah remains on the run from God. The reader is left wondering what will happen next to both the prophet and the Ninevites.

GOD'S CALL AND JONAH'S FLIGHT, 1:1-3

The book of Jonah begins like many of the other prophetic texts: with the word of the Lord coming to the prophet of God (see also Joel 1:1; Mic 1:1; Zeph 1:1; Hag 1:1; Mal 1:1). This formulaic introduction reminds us that prophets do not speak on their own behalf but rather deliver messages that have been revealed to them by God. Prophets are not automatons, however. Moses protests his call three times (Exod 3:11, 4:1, 10). Habakkuk doubts the justice of God's message (Hab 1:12-13). Jeremiah gets so fed up with the life of prophecy that he accuses God of deceit and curses the day he was born (Jer 20:7, 14-15). None of these examples, however, prepares the reader for the extreme measures Jonah will take to resist the call of God on his life.

The text identifies Jonah as the son of Amittai, connecting him with the prophet of the same name in 2 Kings 14:25 who served the northern kingdom during the time of Jeroboam II (786–746 BCE). Little is known about Jonah except that he was born in Gath-Hepher, a town fifteen miles west of the Sea of Galilee (Josh 19:13) near the modern village of Meshed. A contemporary of Amos and Hosea, Jonah delivered a message of grace to an evil king. Evil kings rarely received good news from God's prophets. Usually, they heard messages of condemnation, but Jonah assured Jeroboam II that God would expand the borders of Israel under his reign despite the evil he had done. The oddity of Jonah's message to Jeroboam II sets an interesting backdrop to the book of Jonah. Historically, Jonah's reputation as a prophet suffered as a result of his generous message to an evil king. Could that be one of the reasons this same prophet will struggle to deliver a similar message of grace to an evil and also foreign people? Certainly, the character of Jonah provides an interesting foil to the classic image of an obedient prophet.

Jonah's call to arise and go to Nineveh stands out among the other prophetic calls in the Hebrew Scriptures. God called other prophets to prophesy against foreign nations. For instance, the books of Amos, Obadiah, Nahum, Zechariah, and Malachi all contain oracles against Israel's enemies. While these prophets spoke against foreign powers, they spoke the curses to the people of Judah and Israel. The aim of their words was not to warn a foreign power of God's impending wrath but

---

The Deuteronomistic Historian and Jeroboam's Expansion

The expansion of territory under Jeroboam II (786–746) presents a theological enigma for the Deuteronomistic Historian (the editor of the books of Joshua, Judges, Samuel, and Kings). On the one hand, the historian condemns Jeroboam for failing to turn Israel from its sin of false worship. On the other hand, if Jeroboam was so evil, why did God reward him with expanded territory, a lengthy reign, and economic prosperity? No texts explain this tension. By the time of Josephus (c. 37–100 CE), traditions about Jonah's role had expanded to include specific commands given by YHWH in order to expanded Israel's territory by working through Jonah the prophet to the king:

In the fifteenth year of the reign of Amaziah, Jeroboam the son of Joash reigned over Israel in Samaria forty years. This king was guilty of contumely against God, and became very wicked in worshipping of idols, and in many undertakings that were absurd and foreign. He was also the cause of ten thousand misfortunes to the people of Israel. Now one Jonah, a prophet, foretold to him that he should make war with the Syrians, and conquer their army, and enlarge the bounds of his kingdom on the northern parts to the city Hamath, and on the southern to the lake Asphaltitis; for the bounds of the Canaanites originally were these, as Joshua their general had determined them. So Jeroboam made an expedition against the Syrians, and overran all their country, as Jonah had foretold. (*Antiquities*, Book 9 §10.1)

The prophet is thus given credit for enlarging the territory in Jeroboam's time according to Josephus, and the king's sins are described in more graphic detail.

to encourage Israel that their neighbors' sins would not go unpunished. Jonah's call is different. God says to him, "Go at once to Nineveh, the great city" (v. 2). He is the only minor prophet who prophesies to a foreign people instead of to the people of God. The purpose of Jonah's call is ambiguous. While he is called to cry against Nineveh, the fact that Nineveh is given any notice hints that God might have plans other than judgment for its people.

Nineveh sat on the east side of the Tigris River near the modern city of Mosul in Iraq. The city is called "great" four times over the course of the book of Jonah (1:2; 3:2; 3:3; and 4:11). The repetition of this description brings to mind an expansive city. Nineveh would eventually become one of the largest cities in Mesopotamia. Most of this growth took place after the time of Jonah. Sennacherib (705–681 BCE), king of Assyria, made Nineveh his capital in 701 BCE. Even at its height, however, Nineveh was far smaller than its description in 3:3. There the reader learns that it would take three days to walk across the city. In reality, archaeological digs have revealed a city wall that is only seven and one-half miles around.[1] The descriptions of Nineveh in the book of Jonah likely reveal a late composition of the text. Memories of Assyria's destruction of the northern kingdom haunted Jews for centuries. Over time, the memory of Nineveh's reputation and influence grew so that it far exceeded the city's actual size.

What the author does not exaggerate is Nineveh's wickedness. The Assyrians conquered with overwhelming military might and delighted in torturing their victims. Their propensity for evil is reflected in the near universal derision directed at them in both biblical and non-biblical texts. The prophet Nahum delights in Nineveh's destruction. A Greek maxim from the sixth century BCE read, "A prudent city riding a rock is better than stupid Nineveh that has been destroyed."[2] Nineveh's wickedness meant that almost no one was sad to see her go.

The wickedness of Nineveh and the animosity it generated in response set the stage for the conflict that quickly arises in the book of Jonah. God's call to Jonah is clear. He is to cry out against the city, for their wickedness has come before God. At first glance, the language appears to echo Genesis 4:10, where Abel's blood calls out to the Lord following his murder at the hand of Cain. Throughout the Scriptures, the blood of innocent victims cries out to God for a response. One would expect God to respond to Nineveh's wickedness with punishment and for a prophet of Israel to delight in being selected to

> **Nahum 3:1-4; 18-19**
>
> 📖   Ah! City of bloodshed,
>   utterly deceitful, full of booty—
> no end to the plunder!
> The crack of whip and rumble of wheel,
> galloping horse and bounding chariot!
> Horsemen charging,
> flashing sword and glittering spear,
> piles of dead,
> heaps of corpses,
> dead bodies without end—
> they stumble over the bodies!
> Because of the countless debaucheries of the
> prostitute,
> gracefully alluring, mistress of sorcery,
> who enslaves[a] nations through her debaucheries,
> and peoples through her sorcery . . . .
> Your shepherds are asleep,
> O king of Assyria;
> your nobles slumber.
> Your people are scattered on the mountains
> with no one to gather them.
> There is no assuaging your hurt,
> your wound is mortal.
> All who hear the news about you
> clap their hands over you.
> For who has ever escaped
> your endless cruelty? (NRSV)

deliver that message of doom to a despised enemy. Expectations are put on hold, however, with Jonah's response. Instead of obeying God's call or even arguing with it, Jonah immediately flees in the other direction to Tarshish by way of Joppa (1:3).

At this point, the reader does not know why Jonah flees from God's call. One who does not know the rest of the story (see 4:2) may speculate. Maybe Jonah is afraid of the Ninevites. Their wickedness, after all, knows no bounds. They do not appear to be the kind of people who would receive a foreign prophet with open arms. Maybe Jonah feels he is not up to the task. Other prophets, Moses and Jeremiah for example, doubted their ability to carry out God's plans. Any guess at this point in the story would be conjecture. Jonah does not speak. He only runs. The text does reveal that Jonah puts everything he has into his flight. God called on Jonah to "Go at once to Nineveh." The Hebrew contains with it the idea of getting up and going. For instance, the CEB has "Get up and go to Nineveh." Now Jonah goes down to Joppa, a coastal city near modern-day Jaffa. The wordplay between "Get up" and Jonah going down to Joppa is intentional. "Get up" will appear again in 1:6. Down will reappear in 1:5 and 2:6. The point is clear. Jonah does not simply ignore God's call. Jonah actively flees God's assignment.

Jonah's ultimate destination highlights this fact. In Joppa, he buys a ticket and boards a ship destined for Tarshish, a city in modern-day Spain. Tarshish was about as far from Nineveh as one could get in the known world. The author repeats the final destination three times in verse 3, emphasizing the lengths to which Jonah was willing to go to escape the call of God on his life. More than escaping the call, the text twice tells us that Jonah's flight was an attempt to escape the very presence of the Lord. The illogical nature of this effort is apparent from the start to everyone but Jonah.

A STORMY CONVERSATION, 1:4-16

The remainder of chapter 1 chronicles Jonah's failed attempt to flee from the presence of the Lord. The author uses these verses to set up the main theological points of the book. Jonah, the prophet of God, will resist God's work in the world while pagan sailors prove responsive. For most of the chapter, Jonah is a passive participant. God is the one who acts, and the sailors react. But Jonah remains silent. Ironically, pagan sailors play the role of prophet. They show proper fear of the storm, viewing it as a sign of divine anger. They seek the reason a god may have been angered. They converse with Jonah, highlighting the futility of his flight. They attempt to show mercy to Jonah even though his actions have put them in peril. In the end, they worship God while Jonah sinks in the sea. Ironically, Jonah's disobedience contributes to the salvation of a foreign people despite his reluctance to do God's will. This episode anticipates the action in chapter 3 when an entire city of foreigners will be converted through Jonah's only slightly less reluctant actions.

The Sailors React to the Storm, 1:4-6

The foolishness of Jonah's flight becomes immediately apparent. The boat has barely left the harbor when the Lord hurls a great wind upon the sea. God's action makes clear what any faithful Jew already knew. While God may meet God's people in a special way at the temple in Jerusalem, there is nowhere that one can go to escape God's presence (see Ps 139:7-12). As the maker of heaven and earth, God is not confined to space or time. All the earth remains under God's divine control. The wind is not the only thing God will send in this story. By the end of the book, the wind, the fish, the plant, the worm, and another wind will all do God's bidding. God may grant Jonah the freedom to respond as he pleases, but this does not mean God will refrain from influencing his flight. It seems that God will employ all of nature to help Jonah correct his course.

Throughout the Bible, God uses the wind as an agent of divine work in the world. In the Noah story, God sent a wind to dry the earth and bring salvation to Noah and his family. Here, God sends a wind that threatens Jonah and the sailors on the ship with death. The author highlights the severity of the storm with language that borders on personification. One can translate verse 4, "the ship thought it would break apart."[3] The ship is not the only one who thinks it is in trouble. The seasoned sailors respond to the storm with fear. They have witnessed bad storms before. The reader can assume that extreme weather does not easily unsettle these men, but they recognize this storm as a genuine threat to their lives.

Their fear motivates them to action. First, each sailor cries out to his own god. That each sailor has his own god indicates the presence of a multinational crew. Beyond praying, they begin to hurl the cargo overboard (1:5). The word for "hurl" is the same verb used in verse 4. God "hurled" a wind. The sailors "hurl" the cargo in response. Some commentators suggest that the tossed cargo may have served as sacrifices to the foreign gods, but the text reports a more pragmatic purpose of lightening the load. Either way, the sailors' actions point to the severity of their situation. The cargo represents the very purpose of their journey. Without cargo, they will not get paid. Of course, dead men do not draw a paycheck either.

In complete contrast to the sailors, Jonah remains unmoved by the storm. He continues to move in the opposite direction of God's command to arise and go up to Nineveh by going down into the ship's hull. There he falls asleep (1:6). The Hebrew word indicates a deep sleep. Jonah is experiencing no fear or anxiety as a result of the storm. What is worse, he is experiencing no fear or guilt over his flight from God. He is content in his disobedience. The captain of

Wind

AΩ In Hebrew the word for wind, *rûaḥ*, is the same word as the word for spirit. The gender of *rûaḥ* is feminine in either case. Only the context allows one to decide which is meant. The imagery, however, is instructive for comparing the biblical God to foreign gods in the ancient context. God's spirit does not take human form, nor is it a separate deity. Old Testament texts do not articulate a doctrine of the trinity, though they do contain imagery that forms the background for the development of the doctrine. God's spirit, like the wind, is presented as a mysterious entity that allows God to communicate with humans in a special way (cf. Joel 2:28 [MT 3:1]) or to accomplish a special purpose (Exod 31:3). It is also presumed to be that which dwells within human beings to separate them from the animal world (cf. Gen 6:3 as an interpretation of 2:7) or serves to present God's nurturing presence in the world (Gen 1:2).

the ship, however, is not content with Jonah's inaction. He confronts Jonah by asking him to explain his sleeping. He then calls on Jonah to get up and pray.

The sailors' actions, epitomized by the captain's conversation with Jonah, give us our first glimpse at the ironic thrust of the book. Without realizing what he is doing, the captain says words to Jonah that echo those of the Almighty: "Get up!" Jonah's presence in the bottom of the boat reminds the reader that he is still on the lam, doing everything in his power to flee from God's presence. He has not arisen but has gone down to Joppa and then down into the hull of this ship bound for Tarshish. The pagan sailors, on the other hand, do everything in their power to seek God's saving mercy. They pray and they hope that God, whomever that god might be, will spare their lives. The captain recognizes that God does not have to think of them, but he holds out the possibility that God may show mercy to those who call on his name (1:6). This is why he wants all the men, including Jonah, to offer prayers to their gods. The captain's hope anticipates the hope that the king of Nineveh will show when he later prays, "Who knows? God may relent and change his mind . . . so that we do not perish?" (3:9).

Casting Lots

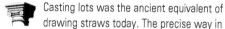 Casting lots was the ancient equivalent of drawing straws today. The precise way in which lots were cast in Old Testament times is not clear, perhaps because the practice varied from place to place and from time to time. A few texts indicate that the lots were cast into someone's lap (e.g., Prov 16:33), but it is not clear what happened then. What is clear is that the assumption that lies behind the practice is that the deity will control the outcome so that a proper decision can be reached, whether that decision concerns who gets what land (Num 26:55-56), spoils (Obad 11), or prisoners (Nah 3:10).

The Sailors Seek the Reason for the Storm, 1:7-10

The text fails to report Jonah's response. His silence may indicate that he remains as unmoved by the captain's words as he was by the Lord's. Instead of dwelling on the prophet, the story shifts once again to the sailors' actions. Apparently, their attempts to lighten the load have failed to ease threat of sinking. They assume that an angry god has caused the storm, but they do not know which god is angry. They turn next to the ancient practice of casting lots to determine who has brought this evil upon them by angering a god (1:7). English translations obscure the fact that the word for evil or calamity in verse 7 is the same word used in verse 2 to describe the Ninevites. Jonah now finds himself guilty of causing evil to befall on others in much the same way as the Assyrians had.

The lot falls on Jonah, tipping the sailors off to what readers already know. The blame belongs with Jonah. The fact that the sailors do not throw him overboard immediately is the first of several signs that these are honorable men. Instead, they pepper him with questions: "Tell us why this calamity has come upon us. What is your occupation? Where do you come from? What is your country? From what people are you?" (1:8). Though Jonah only answers the last question, the sailors' expanded knowledge of his motivation for fleeing in verse 10 indicates that he gave a more thorough answer than is recorded.

Jonah's truncated answer is enough to move the action forward. He replies that he is a Hebrew who worships the God of heaven, the one who made the sea and the dry land. Jonah's answer is confessional. His flight from God does not change the fact that he is a Hebrew, one of God's people. His confession highlights the fact that the prophet is currently at odds with the God whom he worships. Jonah's use of the Lord's personal name highlights Jonah's continued connection to the covenant people of Israel. As a faithful Jew, Jonah has inside information about this God who can move the seas. For instance, he knows that God is not a tribal deity. Instead, he explains that his God is the "God of heaven, who made the sea and the dry land" (v. 9). This language is doxological. It provides a succinct description of God's universal power and reach. The phrase "God of heaven" is not common but does show up in Genesis 24:7; 2 Chronicles 36:23; Ezra 1:2; and Nehemiah 1:5. "God of heaven" is a title that recalls the Jewish belief that they worshiped the one, true God, the creator of the universe. That Jonah specifically mentions God creating the sea and the dry land recalls the language of both creation and the exodus. In creation, God separated the waters and formed the dry land (Gen 1:9-10). God has exerted control over the waters ever since (Exod 14:16-29; Josh 3:14-17). Even though Jonah is fleeing God's command, he does not disown his relationship with the Lord. He goes so far as to say that he worships this God. The word "worship" can also be translated "revere," "stand in awe," or even "fear."[4] It is the appropriate attitude that one is to have before the Lord.

This confession is the first time Jonah has spoken. His words give the reader the first hint that Jonah believes the Lord, his God, has caused this storm in response to his own flight. Jonah's answer sits in the middle of this section, allowing it to act as a hinge in the action. Before Jonah's confession, the sailors had remained in the dark about their troubles. Now these troubles have been brought into the light. Jonah's words may be spoken under duress, but he speaks truth nonetheless. The sailors' ignorance of the Jewish God has now been erased. Through Jonah's confession, they have been introduced to the God of all creation who exerts divine control over both land and sea. Increased knowledge does not lessen their fear. In fact, they grow even more afraid (1:10). Verse 10 reads that the sailors "fear a great fear." In other words, they fear

---

Literary Structure of Jonah 1

📖 Note the artistically arranged structure.

Narrative introduction (1:1-3): Jonah goes from land to sea after hearing YHWH's command

A	Narrative and fear motif (1:4, 5aa)
B	Prayer of sailors (5ab)
C	Narrative (5bc, 6aa)
D	Speech of the captain (6ab, b)
E	Speech of the Sailors 1 (7a)
F	Narrative (7b)
G	Speech of the sailors 2 (8)
Center	Confession of Jonah and fear motif (9, 10aa)
G'	Speech of the sailors 2 (10ab, b)
F'	Narrative (10c)
E'	Speech of the Sailors 1 (11)
D'	Speech of Jonah (12)
C'	Narrative (13)
B'	Prayer of the sailors (with text) (14)
A'	Narrative and fear motif (15, 16)

Narrative transition (2:1f., 11): Jonah goes from sea to land to hear YHWH's command

For analysis of this structure, see James D. Nogalski, *Redactional Processes in the Book of the Twelve* (Beihefte zur Zeitschrift für die alttestamentliche Wissenschaft 218; Berlin: de Gruyter, 1993) 250–55.

---

not simply the storm but also the anger of the God who has caused it. In their fear, they express complete exasperation with Jonah: "What is this that you have done?" The sailors' fear serves to heighten the irony of the story. They have only partial knowledge of God, yet they show reverence and fear. Jonah, as both a Hebrew and a prophet of the Lord, has a much fuller understanding of who God is, claims to worship the Lord, yet acts with disregard toward God's call and remains complacent in the face of God's anger.

The Sailors Attempt to Stop the Storm, 1:11-16

The author alerts us to the fact that the threat of the storm continues to increase (1:11). It may seem strange that the sailors would ask Jonah for help, but they recognize that he is the one with the pertinent information. The sailors know that Jonah's God has been offended. Only Jonah, then, knows what might appease this angry deity. Jonah replies without hesitation. They are to "hurl" him into the sea (1:12). God hurled the wind upon the sea. The sailors hurled the cargo into the sea. Now, Jonah knows that it is his turn. He is the only cargo that needs to be hurled into the ocean. Only his life will calm the sea, for, by his own admission, he is the reason for this storm. This confession is the closest Jonah gets to admitting guilt. His words are not, however, a sign of repentance. They are closer to resignation. Jonah could have suggested that the sailors row him back to Joppa so that he could belatedly answer the call of God. He does not do so. He is not yet ready to obey the Lord. He is not yet ready to see the word of the Lord make its way to Nineveh. He would rather die than obey. Jonah knows that being thrown into the stormy sea is a death sentence.

That he is willing to die alone at least indicates that he does not bear hatred in his heart for all Gentiles as some interpreters of this book have argued. If Jonah hated all Gentiles, he would have been happy to have gone down with the ship, sailors and all. Instead, he recognizes that the Gentile sailors bear no responsibility for this storm. There is no reason for innocent people to die. Jonah's sense of justice is intact. In chapter 4, the reader will learn that an argument with God about what is just and right has led Jonah to this spot in the first place (4:2). Jonah continues to argue with God, but he is not willing for his argument with God to cause others' deaths. Neither is he ready to give in to God's point of view. Jonah is still running from God when he says, "Throw me into the sea."

While Jonah might be ready to die, the sailors are not quite ready to kill him. The text is clear that the sailors do everything possible to avoid throwing Jonah into the sea. They row as hard as they can in an attempt to bring the ship safely back to the harbor, but the storm grows even more fierce, frustrating their valiant efforts. Most English translations again obscure the personification of the sea, which is said to be walking and storming. In their efforts to fight the sea, the sailors show remarkable restraint once more. We learn from verse 14 that they fear they will be held liable for Jonah's death on the off chance that Jonah might be more innocent than he seems. The presentation of these sailors stands as one of the few positive depictions of foreigners in all of prophetic literature. Elsewhere, foreigners are portrayed as idolatrous, wicked evildoers. Here, they are thoughtful, gracious, and reverent. They prove willing to risk their own lives to give Jonah one more chance to live. That is more than Jonah has done so far for the Ninevites.

When it finally becomes clear that throwing Jonah into the sea is their only option, the sailors cry out to the Lord in prayer. They seek the mercy of

Prayer in Jonah 1:14

The excellent studies of P. D. Miller and S. E. Balentine in the 1990s have illuminated the wide variety of forms of prayer in the Hebrew Bible. In terms of form, the sailors' prayer in Jonah 1:14 represents a simple petitionary prayer comprised of three common elements: (1) specific address of the deity (twice YHWH is mentioned specifically); (2) petition (one petition expressed in two ways); (3) motivation (for you . . . have done as you pleased). These elements represent the structural building blocks of the most common type of prayer (Miller, 57). Nevertheless, the common structure should not obscure the fact that the prayer of the sailors in 1:14 is contextual, drawing upon the character and the situation of Jonah 1. This contextual characteristic sets the sailors' prayer apart from Jonah's prayer in 2:2-9, which seems to presuppose a setting quite different from its literary context. Concerning the functionality of contextual prayers, see Balentine, pages 18–19. The function of the two prayers is also noteworthy. Balentine (267) notes that prayer serves two primary functions with regard to characterizing humans: (1) emphasizing essential qualities of faith and (2) providing a lens upon piety by which to judge the characters' actions. In the case of the sailors' prayer, the sailors display a recognition of YHWH's power that motivates their prayer, and their actions are portrayed as consistent with the piety of their prayer. The sailors attempt to avoid harming Jonah before they pray, and after their prayer they make a sacrifice and pay vows (1:16). By contrast, Jonah's prayer in 2:2-9 presents the words of a pious individual who turns to YHWH for help in time of great distress, but the continuation of the narrative casts a negative light on Jonah's piety because he only reluctantly completes his mission, and then spars with YHWH because YHWH has shown compassion on the foreigners. Prayers by foreigners are not common in the Old Testament, so the fact that the sailors pray at all is already unusual. The fact that the sailors serve as a model of piety while Jonah's prayer highlights his petulance as the narrative continues only heightens the contrast between the prophets and the foreign sailors.

Patrick D. Miller, *They Cried to the Lord: The Form and Theology of Biblical Prayer* (Minneapolis: Fortress, 1994).

Samuel E. Balentine, *Prayer in the Hebrew Bible: The Drama of Divine-Human Dialogue* (OBT; Minneapolis: Fortress, 1993).

Jonah's God, even as they toss Jonah into the sea. They become one of the few foreigners in all the Bible to address Israel's God by the divine name. Upon completing their prayer, they throw Jonah into the waters. Immediately the sea stops raging. The miraculous calming of the waters causes them to fear Jonah's God even more. The disciples' response to Jesus' calming of the storm gives us a glimpse into the sailors' inner thoughts. Mark 4:41 reports that when the disciples witnessed Jesus' calming of the sea, "They were terrified and asked each other, 'Who is this? Even the wind and the waves obey him!'" (NIV). No doubt, the sailors wondered what kind of God this was who could stir the sea into a rage and calm it to a whisper in a moment's notice. They respond in the only way one should respond, by worshiping this mighty God. In awe, they offer sacrifices and make vows to the God of Jonah. Meanwhile, Jonah sinks into the deep. He has contributed to the conversion of the pagan sailors despite himself. They have been saved. The reader is left wondering, "Will anyone save Jonah?"

TEACHING THIS CHAPTER

The book of Jonah is a wonderful example of the power of a good beginning. With a few short verses, the author of Jonah grabs the readers' attention and prepares us for a wild ride. Throughout this first chapter, the author of Jonah delights even the casual reader with humor, irony, and careful wordplay. This author has done more than entertain. Jonah's story engages readers with two captivating topics. First, the plot of this chapter allows us to explore the tension between God's sovereignty and human freedom. Second, the chapter holds forth the surprising possibility that outsiders might be more open to God's work in the world than insiders. Both of these themes provide ample material for a lesson that captures the attention of modern readers.

A lesson that explores the tension between God's sovereignty and human freedom should begin by acknowledging that the book of Jonah, along with the rest of the Hebrew Scriptures, presents the Lord as a sovereign God who engages humanity. In chapter 1, God's sovereignty is on display in the fact that nature bends to the divine will, and this is elegantly described in Jonah's confession: "I worship the LORD, the God of heaven, who made the sea and the dry land." God's sovereignty is also on display in the fact that God reveals the divine word to Jonah. It is easy to pass over this verse, but an important truth can be found here. Human beings cannot discover the divine word on their own. Nor can human beings manipulate God into revealing the word. People have access to God's word only through divine revelation. The good news of the biblical narrative is that God graciously shows up in the human story and reveals the divine word for humanity's benefit.

Equally remarkable is the fact that when God shows up, over and over again, God invites human beings not only to hear but also to participate in the divine work. God does not write the divine word in the clouds above Nineveh. Instead, God instead calls Jonah to deliver the word of God to the Ninevites. Notice that God does not force Jonah to go to Nineveh. Jonah is free to accept or reject the call. Jonah's freedom to choose does not contradict God's sovereignty. Though God could force Jonah's hand, God grants Jonah the freedom to respond. Our ability to choose obedience or disobedience results from God's gracious willingness to let us choose. The fact that God allows us free choice does not mean that God sits idly by as we make disobedient choices. God pursues Jonah, employing all of nature to cajole Jonah toward repentance. The storm, though violent, is a form of grace that slows Jonah's journey into disobedience. As Barth reminds us, "Grace is patient. But grace is also stormy."[5] By the end of chapter 1, God's efforts have not proved fruitful in Jonah's life, but the point has been made that God will not give up on Jonah or the Ninevites without a fight.

God's call of Jonah reminds the reader that God consistently invites human beings to join in the divine work. The teacher has more connecting points in the Scriptures than can be listed here. One path could involve comparing and contrasting the call stories of other Old Testament prophets including Moses (Exod 3:1-11), Jeremiah (Jer 1:4-6), and Isaiah (Isa 6:1-8). Another would be to explore Jesus' invitation both to those who respond favorably (Mark 1:16-20; 2:14) and to those who do not (Mark 10:17-22; Luke 9:57-62). None of these are exact parallels to Jonah's flight, but they provide the reader with a variety of examples to draw from when discussing both God's call on the believer's life and human responses. The teacher could ask students to elaborate on the reasons people today flee from God's call in their lives. A class could also explore the variety of methods we use to flee from God's presence. Often people are actively fleeing from God's presence even as they sit in the pews of their local church.

God's pursuit of Jonah brings to mind Francis Thompson's Victorian-era poem "The Hound of Heaven." In this poem, the narrator flees from God "down the nights and down the days . . . down the arches of the years . . . down the labyrinthine ways." No matter where he goes or how ardently he hides, God pursues him "with unhurrying chase, and unperturbed pace." The late John Stott referenced Thompson's poem when he admitted, "[My faith is] due to Jesus Christ himself, who pursued me relentlessly even when I was running away from him in order to go my own way. And if it were not for the gracious pursuit of the hound of heaven I would today be on the scrap-heap of wasted and discarded lives."[6] Other Christians have echoed these thoughts. God gives us the freedom to reject the divine call on our lives, but that does not mean that God leaves men and women to their own disobedience. God pursues us.

Initially, that pursuit can feel oppressive (see Ps 32:4). The common declaration that "The Lord is near" can be taken as either a warning or a comfort. The teacher can invite students to share times when they felt pursued by the very presence of the God whom they were attempting to flee.

Another approach the teacher can take to chapter 1 focuses more on the contrast between Jonah and the sailors. From the first couple of verses, the author of Jonah asks the reader to revisit the question, "Who is most open to God's action in the world?" The default answer for the original readers of Jonah would be that Jews, as God's people, were most open to God's work in the world. Much of the Hebrew Scriptures present God as a universal God who is sovereign over all the peoples of the earth. That being said, the narrative thrust of the Old Testament is that this universal God has a special relationship with God's people, the Jews. Solomon's prayer at the dedication of the temple serves as a good summary of the Jews' self-understanding: "For you have separated [Israel] from among all the peoples of the earth, to be your heritage, just as you promised through Moses, your servant, when you brought our ancestors out of Egypt, O Lord God" (1 Kgs 8:53). This meant Israel had access to God, symbolized by the temple, that other nations did not.

If the relationship between Israel and the Lord is clear in the Hebrew Scriptures, God's relationship with the nations is more ambiguous. Some texts clearly take an antagonistic stance toward outsiders. In Joshua and Judges, the Canaanites are to be either driven from the land or exterminated altogether. In Ezra and Nehemiah, foreigners are expelled from Jerusalem, including the foreign wives and children of Jewish men. And in most of the prophets, foreigners are viewed as enemies of God's people destined for destruction. A handful of texts in the Hebrew Bible view foreigners more favorably. The Law clearly makes provisions for the foreigner living among the Jews (Lev 19:10, 33, 34; 23:22; 24:22). In the prayer of dedication mentioned above, Solomon holds out hope that foreign peoples will one day look to the temple and worship the God of Israel (1 Kgs 8:41-43). The prophet Isaiah builds on this idea and foresees a day when God's work in Israel will serve as a beacon to the world: "The nations will come to your light, and kings to the brightness of your dawn" (Isa 60:3). Again, the majority of the Hebrew Scriptures view foreigners with suspicion, if not outright disdain, but a handful of texts hold a more favorable view.

The book of Jonah fits with the minority of voices that see foreigners as people capable of responding to God's work in the world. The character of

Jonah serves as a case study for how these competing voices concerning the relationship of foreigners to Israel's God might play out in the life of an individual Jew. It is noteworthy that the author nowhere labels Jonah a prophet in this book. Jonah is, in many ways, representative of Israel as a whole. Even his name, Jonah, which means dove, is often used as a not-so-flattering symbol for Israel at large (Ps 74:19; Hos 7:11; 11:11). Jonah represents an Israel that struggles with its role of being a light to the nations. It is not that Jonah despises all foreigners; he does not.

> **Theology of Exclusion**
>
> The Hebrew Bible is not of one voice when it comes to its relationship with the nations, though one is more widely represented. A major strand in the Former and Latter Prophets displays a decisively antagonistic stance toward those outside Israel and Judah. Joshua and Judges expect foreigners to be annihilated from the land (e.g., Josh 1:2-5; 12–22; Judg 2:1-5), though the difficulty of doing so is never resolved (see Judg 3:1-5). All four of the Latter Prophets contain collections of oracles directed against foreign nations (Isa 13–23; Jer 46–51; Ezek 25–32; Amos 1–2; Obadiah; Nahum; and Habakkuk). Postexilic narratives (Ezra, Nehemiah, and Chronicles) largely follow this antagonistic strand. One finds this negative attitude illustrated particularly clearly in Ezra and Nehemiah, where acts of exclusion manifest themselves in official policies such as forcing Judean men to divorce their foreign wives (Ezra 10) and correlating loyalty to God with not marrying foreigners (Neh 10:28-31). This theology of exclusion is largely driven by ideas of purity (religious and ethnic) and fear. For further reading, see Miroslav Volf, *Exclusion and Embrace: A Theological Exploration of Identity, Otherness, and Reconciliation* (Nashville: Abingdon, 1996) and Joel S. Kaminsky, *Yet I Loved Jacob: Reclaiming the Biblical Concept of Election* (Nashville: Abingdon, 2007).

Jonah gets along with the sailors well enough. Furthermore, he is headed to Tarshish, a Gentile city. Eugene Peterson points out that Jonah may even think he can get away with ministering there instead of in Nineveh.[7] Jonah is willing to arise and go to some Gentiles. He just cannot bring himself to arise and go to those Gentiles in Nineveh. It is not the going to foreigners that Jonah resists. It is this particular group of foreigners that Jonah despises. Their violence and wickedness give him good reasons for disliking them.

Jonah's case drives home the challenge of being the person or group of people whom God calls to shine as a light to the nations. If God means all nations, then eventually God will call someone from among God's people to be a light to the nations who are despised most of all. Isaiah certainly thought that God's ultimate plans included all the peoples of the earth. The book of Jonah appears to support this vision. As Fretheim notes, "If God is concerned that his Word be heard in Nineveh, of all places, he must care enough about his world to want it to be heard everywhere."[8] God's people can come up with any number of reasons not to answer the call to deliver God's word to some people. We may assume that certain people do not want to hear the word of God. What the story of Jonah suggests is that those we least expect to be open to the word of the Lord may be more ready to hear that word than even the people of God are. This truth comes to fruition in the life and ministry of first Jesus Christ and then the Apostle Paul. Jesus met with great resistance among the religious elites of his day but noted that the prostitutes and tax collectors were having no trouble finding their way into the kingdom of God (Matt 21:31-32). Paul managed to convert some Jews, but his ministry grew exponentially among Gentiles. More sinister than assuming some do not want to hear God's word is the belief that some people do not deserve to receive God's word. This is probably closer to Jonah's objection concerning the Ninevites. We will explore this objection in chapter 4. A teacher could explore the various groups of people whom we think are undeserving of God's mercy.

The faithful response of the sailors in the first chapter of Jonah antici-pates the openness of outsiders to the gospel of Jesus Christ. Sailors, in the ancient world as much as in ours, were not known for piety. And yet these sailors proved open to God's work in the world in ways that Jonah did not. They prayed when Jonah did not. Jonah claimed to worship God, but the sailors actually did. In many ways, they embodied the Jewish understanding of wisdom. They feared God. Sure, at first they feared the storm. Psalm 29 reminds us that storms can create within us a holy sense of fear that is one step away from worship. The sailors make that step as soon as they are given the most basic information about the one true God. Their lives serve as living examples of Proverbs 9:10, "The fear of the LORD is the beginning of wisdom, and the knowledge of the Holy One is insight." Jonah, on the other hand, has no fear of the Lord and even less wisdom. His attempt to flee the presence of the Lord has led him into the depths of the sea. If he could not escape God down in Joppa or down in the bottom of the boat, what makes him think he will escape God's presence down in the bottom of the sea? Questions about how outsiders might be more ready to hear a word from the Lord than insiders might prove fertile ground for class discussion.

QUESTIONS FOR REFLECTION AND DISCUSSION

1. Jonah flees the call of God without saying a word, leaving the reader unclear as to his reasons for running. What might be some of the reasons Jonah ran from God's presence? Why do we sometimes seek to avoid the presence of the Lord?

2. Why do you think the author of Jonah chose to keep Jonah's motivation for fleeing God's presence a secret until the end of the book?

3. God grants Jonah the freedom to disobey. This does not mean that God leaves Jonah alone in his disobedience. How did God intervene in Jonah's life? How does God intervene in our lives when we disobey?

4. Throughout chapter 1, the pagan sailors prove more open to the work of God than Jonah does. Where have you seen this play out in modern life? When and how do outsiders sometimes seem more responsive to God's leading than those already inside the church?

5. Fear plays a major role in the sailors' journey toward God. How can fear be a positive force in our relationship with God? How can fear sometimes be destructive to our relationship with God?

SUGGESTIONS FOR WORSHIP AND PREACHING

Order of Worship

Prelude

Call to Worship
Almighty King and Merciful Lord,
Speak to us your Living Word,
A word of correction.
A word of grace.
A word of life.
Amen.

"Come, Thou Almighty King"

Welcome and Greeting

"Come Thou Fount of Every Blessing"

"Great Is Thy Faithfulness" (Thomas O. Chisholm, 1923. Renewal 1951, Hope Publishing)

Responsive Reading from Psalm 139
Where can I go from your spirit?
Or where can I flee from your presence?
If I ascend to heaven,
You are there;
If I make my bed in Sheol,
You are there;
If I take the wings of the morning
and settle at the farthest limits of the sea,
Even there your hand shall lead me,
and your right hand shall hold me fast.
If I say, "Surely the darkness shall cover me,
and the light around me become night,"
Even the darkness is not dark to you;
the night is as bright as day,
for darkness is as light to you.
This is the word of the Lord.
Thanks be to God.

"God Moves in a Mysterious Way" (William Cowper, 1731–1800)

New Testament Reading: Mark 4:35-41

Choral Anthem: "He Will Hold Me Fast" (Original words vv. 1-2 by Ada Habershonnew; additional words by Matt Merker, Getty Music, 2013)

Sermon: You Can Run, but You Can't Hide (Jonah 1:1-16)

Hymn of Invitation: "Precious Lord, Take My Hand" (Thomas Dorsey, Hill & Range, 1938)

Benediction: "Let the word of Christ dwell in you richly; teach and admonish one another in all wisdom; and with gratitude in your hearts sing psalms, hymns, and spiritual songs to God. And whatever you do, in word or deed, do everything in the name of the Lord Jesus, giving thanks to God the Father through him. (Col 3:16-17)

Example Sermon Outline: You Can Run, but You Can't Hide (Jonah 1:1-16)

Introduction

Over the last few years, the number of surveillance cameras in use in the United States has skyrocketed. One estimate puts the number of security cameras purchased in the last decade at around thirty million. That does not include the cameras in our cell phones or the fact that more and more law enforcement agencies chase bad guys with cameras mounted to drones. Add to these ubiquitous cameras the data trail we leave on our computers and cell phones, and you realize that someone is always watching us. The old saying is becoming more and more true: "You can run, but you can't hide." The likelihood of being caught does not keep people from running. Sin has a way of blinding us to the obvious truth.

Reasons for Leaving

We run from God when we cannot stomach his ways. Early in our lives, this happens when we want to indulge in something that God has forbidden. Later in life, after we have followed Christ for a while, we run the temptation of sinning not by indulging in some forbidden fruit but by failing to follow where Jesus leads. God calls us to love our neighbors and pray for our enemies, and we simply pass. We do not actively hurt them, but neither do we go out of our way to help them. God says go and we stay. Sometimes we even run the other way.

When God called Jonah to arise and go up to Ninevah and preach against the city, Jonah fled in the other direction. From a distance, this call to Nineveh seems like a prophet's dream assignment. The people of Nineveh had a reputation for evil, and God wanted Jonah to go and tell them off. Jonah's backstory in 2 Kings 14:25 provides a hint as to his hesitation. There, Jonah obeyed God by bringing a good message to a bad king, Jeroboam II. This was not a normal assignment for a prophet. Prophets usually brought bad messages to bad kings. Instead of doom and gloom, Jonah delivered a message of grace that could not have been popular with the people. Jeroboam II oppressed the people and disobeyed the Lord, and my guess is that people wanted him to get his comeuppance.

Jonah had his suspicions that this trip to Nineveh would be more of the same, only worse. Sure, God wanted him to preach against the city, but why even let the city know that God was upset? After all, no other prophet had ever been asked to go to a foreign city to preach before. Other prophets announced to Israel the fall of foreign nations, and then those nations fell. The nations themselves did not get a warning. As far as Jonah was concerned, fire from heaven was all that would be needed for this job. Why go all the way to Nineveh unless God actually had other plans? Jonah wanted no part of those other plans. It was bad enough giving a good report to a bad king of Israel. But to give a good report to the wicked king of Nineveh was beyond the pale. So Jonah fled.

The Stormy Love of God

When Jonah started running to Joppa, somewhere in the back of his mind, he had to know that this was not going to work. After all, who can escape the presence of the Lord? Even a child knows the answer to that question. Still, Jonah tried. God said, "Get up and go," but Jonah intentionally went *down* in the opposite direction. Down in Joppa, Jonah bought a ticket on a boat headed to Tarshish, a city as far away from Nineveh as one could reasonably get. Jonah's motivation was clear. He did not simply want to get away from God's call. Jonah wanted to get away from God.

Jonah's flight toward Tarshish serves two purposes. In getting as far away from Nineveh as possible, Jonah actively rejects the call of God on his life. In getting as far from Jerusalem as he can, Jonah closes his eyes to all the things that remind him of God. We often do much the same thing when we stop going to church or reading our Bibles in an effort to minimize the chance that God will confront us in our sin. Like Jonah, we cut ourselves off from everything that reminds us of God. Like Jonah, though, we quickly learn that this strategy does not work long-term. While we can actively ignore God, there is nowhere we can run where God cannot find us.

Just because God lets us take off does not mean we have actually escaped from God's care. While God will not force our obedience, neither will he leave us alone in disobedience. C. S. Lewis once noted that hell is where God gives sinners exactly what they want: life without God. Fortunately, God rarely lets us take the freeway to our destruction. Instead, God graciously places plenty of roadblocks in our way. Jonah was supposed to be a roadblock on the Ninevites' journey to ruin. Now God must place obstructions in Jonah's path.

The first roadblock Jonah faces on this journey away from God's presence is a mighty storm. The text reports that God hurled a great wind upon the waters. In Hebrew, the word for spirit and the word for wind is the same. For Elijah, God's voice was not in the storm but rather in the sheer silence. Here, God's spirit is in the storm. I like how the famous theologian Karl Barth once put it: "Grace is patient. But grace is also stormy."[9] What a storm it must have been. It compelled experienced sailors to dump their cargo into the sea and cry out to every god they could name. Jonah, meanwhile, continued to flee the presence of the Lord, going down into the hull of the ship and falling asleep.

In response to Jonah's persistence, God ramps up the storm and recruits some unlikely help: these same pagan sailors. First, the captain comes down into the ship and wakes Jonah up with God's own words, "Get up!" Then this pagan sailor invites Jonah to do the one thing he least wants to do, "Pray." The irony of the situation is thick. Jonah, the prophet, should have gone to pagan Nineveh with the message, "Pray and perhaps the Lord will save us." Instead, it is a pagan man who has to say these words to him.

Even still, Jonah resists. The storm grows stronger and the sailors more tenacious. They cast lots and discover that Jonah is to blame. Only when cornered does he finally admit that the storm is his fault. Even then he does so in an indirect manner, not by expressing guilt but by acknowledging that he worships the only God capable of making a storm like this. He worships "the God of heaven who made the land and the sea."

The sailors are beside themselves. What has Jonah done? Even they can see it's foolish to try to outrun the one who made the sea. They show their desperation by asking Jonah what should be done. Jonah responds simply, "Throw me into the sea."

God Is Ready to Save

It would be a mistake to see Jonah's action as a sign of repentance. After all, he could have asked the sailors to return him to Joppa. Jonah's actions are more a sign of resignation. He is not yet ready to obey the Lord. He is not yet ready to see the word of the Lord make its way to Nineveh. He would rather die than obey. Jonah knows that being thrown into the stormy sea is a death sentence.

Graciously, God puts one more roadblock in his way. The sailors try to row back to Joppa, but to no avail. The presentation of these sailors stands as one of the few positive depictions of foreigners in all of prophetic literature. Elsewhere, foreigners are portrayed as idolatrous, wicked evildoers. Here, they are thoughtful, gracious, and reverent. They prove willing to risk their lives to give Jonah one more chance to live. Even so, Jonah refuses to repent, proving that while we cannot hide from God, we can resist divine grace with simple, stubborn pride.

The scene closes with the sailors hurling Jonah, their last bit of cargo, into the sea. When the winds die down, the sailors respond with awe and fear. Throughout the first chapter, God's actions have aimed to save. God wanted to save the Ninevites. God has tried to save Jonah. The sailors' salvation reveals that Jonah has become a missionary despite himself. Their conversion also emphasizes the fact that God's grace can reach any heart that is humble enough to receive it. Meanwhile, Jonah is quite literally on his way to hell, leaving the reader to wonder, "Does God have any more roadblocks to place in the prophet's way?"

NOTES

1. James Limburg, *Jonah*, Old Testament Library (Louisville KY: Westminster/John Knox, 1993) 40.

2. Jack M. Sasson, *Jonah*, Anchor Bible (New York: Doubleday, 1990) 70.

3. James D. Nogalski, *The Book of the Twelve: Hosea–Jonah*, Smyth & Helwys Bible Commentary (Macon GA: Smyth & Helwys, 2011) 417.

4. Limburg, *Jonah*, 53.

5. Karl Barth, *Here and Now* (New York: Routledge, 1964) 44.

6. Roger Steer, *Basic Christian: The Inside Story of John Stott* (Downers Grove IL: IVP, 2009) 262–63.

7. Eugene H. Peterson, *Under the Unpredictable Plant: An Exploration in Vocational Holiness* (Grand Rapids MI: Eerdmans, 1992) 11.

8. Terence E. Fretheim, *The Message of Jonah* (Minneapolis: Augsburg, 1977) 41.

9. Barth, *Here and Now*, 44.

JONAH PRAYS AND GOD SAVES

Jonah 1:17–2:10

At the end of the first chapter, the author leaves the reader with the image of pagan sailors worshiping the God of Israel on the deck of their boat. Meanwhile, a prophet of Israel sinks in the sea. The story of Jonah could have ended with the prophet's drowning in the sea as a fitting end for a disobedient soul. The reader, after all, has already learned important lessons about God's compassion toward outsiders, God's patience with runaways, and the sad truth that persistent disobedience will nevertheless lead to one's destruction. Fortunately for Jonah, the story does not end there. One loose end remains. What will God do about the Ninevites? God called Jonah to deliver a message to the people of that wicked city. Jonah's disobedience and almost sure death have left that task undone. Will God leave this mission unfinished? No, God will not. God will not give up on the goal of reaching the Ninevites. Remarkably, neither will God give up on reaching Jonah. In Jonah 1:17–2:10, the story of Jonah shifts from *GOOD OPENING* the surface of the sea to its depths. Rather than meeting a certain death, the disobedient prophet meets a great fish that remarkably rescues the sinking soul. In the belly of the fish, Jonah finally speaks to the God he has been fleeing with a psalm of thanksgiving.

DELIVERED BY A FISH, 1:17–2:1

Jonah 1:17–2:1 and 2:10 provide a narrative frame around Jonah's prayer of thanksgiving. In 1:17, the Lord provides a large fish to swallow up the sinking prophet. Then later in 2:10, the Lord speaks to the fish that then spews Jonah onto dry land. For the three days and nights in between, Jonah resides in the belly of the fish. The phrase "three days" is a Hebraic way of communicating a few days' time (Gen 22:4; Exod 3:18; Num 33:8; Josh 2:16; Hab 6:2). In

3 DAYS' MEANING

extra-biblical literature, it was sometimes used to refer to the time required to journey to the underworld.[1] As Jonah's words will indicate, Sheol was precisely the place he was headed until God rescued him via the gulping action of a big fish.

While Jonah spends a significant amount of time in the belly of the fish, the fish plays only a minor role in the story. In 1930, Charles Brown wrote of the disproportionate amount of attention given to the fish:

> It is almost tragic that one of the noblest of the shorter books in the Bible should be known chiefly for its reference to a whale. And the whale only appears in two short verses . . . . He was scarcely more than a bit of stage dressing in that drama of disobedience. Yet for some reason Jonah and the whale are always named together, like David and Jonathan or Romeo and Juliet.[2]

Brown's frustration may be a little overwrought, but his point holds. The main characters of the book are not Jonah and the fish but Jonah and the Lord. Even inside the fish, the focus remains firmly on Jonah's relationship with his God.

One of the reasons for the endless focus on the fish has to do with the strangeness of the story. Another involves the preoccupation of modern readers with the historicity of this story. Scholars, clergy, and laypeople alike have spent copious amounts of ink and conversation in attempts to determine whether or not the reader should view this story literally or not. Attempts to determine whether or not a man could live for three days in the belly of a large fish miss the point of this book. Yes, there are other ancient stories about people surviving inside a fish.[3] Yes, a God who can raise a man from the dead can keep a man alive in a fish. Notably, this book cares little for making such a case. The theme of the book lies elsewhere. Often, arguments about whether this story took place create more heat than light. The simple truth is that Jonah as parable works just as well as Jonah as historical fact. As Jesus' stories prove, parables can be as powerful as miracles for conveying God's truth. Preoccupation with proving our point of view concerning the historicity of this tale tends to distract from the deeper truths of the story.

The Sign of Jonah in the New Testament

Matthew relates Jonah's time in the belly of the fish to the duration of Jesus' time in the tomb (Matt 12:39-40), but Luke relates the sign of Jonah to the behavior of the people of Nineveh, who, unlike the crowds listening to Jesus, repented at the message of Jonah and were spared by God (Luke 11:29-32).

While the fish plays only a minor role, the fish's presence serves an important purpose. Like the storm on the sea, the fish serves as one more indication of how far God will go to extend mercy to the disobedient. If the idea of a man being swallowed by a fish as he sinks into the depths sounds absurd, it is because it is supposed to sound absurd. The author wants us to know that God's mercy toward sinners extends far beyond human expectations. God's compassion makes no logical sense. If God were as pragmatic as we are, God would simply let us perish in our sin. Thankfully, God loves extravagantly, not pragmatically. God will go to all manner of lengths to rescue sinners from their deserved fate. God's actions toward Jonah once again prove the Lord is "a God merciful and gracious, slow to anger, and abounding in steadfast love and faithfulness" (Exod 34:6). As remarkable as it is to think of a man being kept alive in the belly of a fish, God's mercy toward sinners proves even more astounding.

God's rescue of Jonah certainly indicates that God has not yet given up on him. God's rescue of the prophet also hints that God has not yet given up on the Ninevites. Questions remain: How will Jonah respond to God's gracious deliverance? Will Jonah complete the mission to Nineveh? We get our first glimpse of the answer with the simple report that "Jonah prayed to the LORD his God from the belly of the fish" (2:2). Up to this point, Jonah has only spoken *of* God (1:10). Jonah's prayer marks the first time Jonah has spoken *to* God in this entire affair.

JONAH'S PRAYER, 2:2-9

Jonah's prayer takes the form of a thanksgiving song. Other thanksgiving psalms include Psalms 30, 32, 34, 41, 107, and 116. James Mays notes that thanksgiving songs contain three typical elements. First, there is praise addressed to the Lord that rehearses both the cry for help and the Lord's response. Second, there is a summons to the community of faith to join in the praise of God. Third, there is praise made in connection with a vow or sacrifice as an act of thanksgiving.[4] Jonah's song includes an extended recollection of danger and deliverance (2:2-6) and a declaration of praise in connection with a vow (2:7-9). It does not contain an appeal to the congregation to join with Jonah in praising the Lord. The absence of this element may reflect the setting. Usually, psalms of

---

Thanksgiving Song

The consistently appearing elements of the song of thanksgiving have been noted since the time of Hermann Gunkel. Enough of these elements appear in Jonah 2:2-9 so as to leave no real doubt as to how it should be classified. The order and number of these elements varies according to the writer of the song, but the elements themselves are quite consistent in the thanksgiving song. Compare Jonah 2 with Psalm 30, another thanksgiving song:

Elements (Eng. Verse #s)	Psalm 30	Jonah 2
Call to sing (usually addressed to participants in the celebration, or to YHWH)	4-5	
Recounting of the danger and deliverance	3, 6-8	3-6
Profession of YHWH as the deliverer from distress	1-2	2, 7, 9
Announcement of the thanksgiving sacrifice		9
Blessing upon the participants		
Hymnic elements or a didactic element (Gunkel, 205)	5, 9	8
A concluding petition	10-12	

For further reading about thanksgiving songs, see Hermann Gunkel, *Introduction to the Psalms*, §7 "Individual Thanksgiving Songs" (trans. James D. Nogalski; Mercer Library of Biblical Studies; Macon GA: Mercer University Press, 1998) 199–221; see also Erhard Gerstenberger, "Psalms," in *Old Testament Form Criticism* (ed. John H. Hayes; San Antonio: Trinity University Press, 1974) 202–205; for an excellent discussion of the thanksgiving song in Jonah, see James Limburg, *Jonah* (OTL; Louisville: Westminster John Knox, 1993) 64–66.

---

thanksgiving were sung in the presence of a congregation. Jonah sings this song alone in the belly of a fish.

These verses of poetry easily stand out from the rest of the narrative, leading some scholars to argue that the psalm may not have been original to the story. The story reads quite naturally without the psalm: "Then Jonah prayed to the LORD his God from the belly of the fish. Then the LORD spoke to the fish, and it spewed Jonah out upon the dry land." Furthermore, while the psalm has certain similarities to the narrative, the differences are also glaring. The psalm speaks of the Lord, instead of the sailors, throwing Jonah into the sea. The poem does give God credit for saving Jonah but makes no mention of the fish. The psalm is also the only part of the story that portrays Jonah in a positive light. It is possible that a later editor added this psalm to bolster the prophet's reputation in the story. More likely, the original author drew from a preexistent psalm in order to serve his didactic and narrative purposes.

For all the minor discrepancies between the psalm and the narrative, the song does provide a glimpse of what happens to a person who has come face to face with the consequences of his sins, only to then cry out to God and experience a miraculous deliverance. In this way, the poem works well with the

Poems Inserted into Narratives

The insertion of a poem into a narrative is by no means unique to Jonah in the editorial history of the Hebrew Bible. Some prominent examples include Exod 15, where two songs interrupt the narrative to celebrate the exodus event: the song of Moses (15:1-18) and the much shorter song of Miriam (15:20-22). Another song of Moses appears at the end of Deuteronomy, just prior to Moses' death (Deut 32:1-43). The song of Deborah (Judg 5) memorializes the defeat of Sisera.

David's song of thanksgiving in 2 Sam 22 celebrates the exploits of David's life at the point when "the LORD delivered him from the hand of all his enemies, and from the hand of Saul" (22:1). Hezekiah's psalm recounted in Isa 38:9-20 interrupts the conversation between Isaiah and Hezekiah in 38:1-8, 21. For discussions of these and other psalms in this context, see James W. Watts, *Psalm and Story: Inset Hymns in Hebrew Narrative* (Sheffield: JSOT Press, 1992).

---

narrative. Readers hear Jonah's voice in this text, as they should. The author or editor wants the reader to hear Jonah's perspective in this psalm even if it is a preexistent piece. The inclusion of this psalm also allows readers to connect their own stories with the story of Jonah. While it is safe to assume that none of the original readers had spent time in the belly of a fish, it is equally safe to assume that as faithful Jews they had recited a thanksgiving psalm after being delivered from some self-inflicted danger.

Whatever the origin of the psalm, Jonah's prayer from the belly of the fish stands as one of the most enduring images in all of Scripture. Numerous artists have attempted to capture the scene through paintings, drawings, sculptures, and mosaics. One of the most evocative depictions can be found in a few lines from Aldous Huxley's 1917 poem "Jonah."

> Seated upon the convex mound
> Of one vast kidney, Jonah prays
> And sings his canticles and hymns,
> Making the hollow vault resound
> God's goodness and mysterious ways,
> Till the great fish spouts music as he swims.[5]

The book may be about the Lord and the prophet Jonah, but poems like this one make it easy to understand why most people will continue to refer to it as Jonah and the whale.

Fish

Fourth-century Christian mosaic. Note the portrayal of the fish as a sea monster.

Jonah swallowed by the whale. Early Christian mosaic, 4th C. Basilica Patriarcale, Aquileia, Italy. (Credit: Cameraphoto Arte, Venice/ Art Resource, NY)

The entire tale of the book of Jonah is depicted: God commands Jonah to go to Nineveh, Jonah flees by boat, Jonah is swallowed by a big fish, God gives Jonah a second chance, Jonah preaches in Nineveh, and Jonah sits under a vine as a worm begins to eat it.

Martin Luther (1483–1546). "Episodes from the Life of Jonah." *Die Propheten alle deudsch* (1541). (Credit: Courtesy of the Richard C. Kessler Reformation Collection, Pitts Theology Library, Candler School of Theology, Emory University)

Note that the character of the fish is that of a large fish, no longer the mythic monster.

Waclaw Donay (1744–1796). Fountain sculpture on the Market Square in Skoczów, Poland. 18th C. (Credit: Schweppes, http://commons. wikimedia.org/wiki/File:Skoczow_-_Tryton-Jonasz_2009-04-26.jpg)

By the end of the 19th and 20th centuries, artists tended to depict a whale rather than a large fish, as here where the whale appears twice, including once as Jonah prays.

James Lesesne Wells (1902–1993). *Jonah and the Whale.* n.d. Woodcut. Smithsonian American Art Museum, Washington, DC. (Credit: Smithsonian American Art Museum, Washington, DC/ Art Resource, NY)

Depictions of Jonah and the fish appear in paintings, mosaics, and drawings across the centuries. Interestingly, the conceptualization of the fish as a whale is a late development. Through the Middle Ages, two other concepts predominate. Some artists portrayed the fish as a sea monster (perhaps influenced by legends associating the fish with Leviathan; see the top two images). Other artists depicted the fish in less frightening terms merely as an oversized fish (see the image on bottom left). By the end of the nineteenth century, the image of Jonah in a whale begins to dominate (see the image on bottom right).

Jonah Faces the Prospect of Life without God, 2:2-4

The first verse of the psalm serves as a summary of the whole. Jonah cried out to God in his distress, and God answered him. This verse provides the first indication that Jonah spoke to God before being swallowed by the fish. In the first chapter, the captain of the ship directed Jonah to call on his God, but Jonah remained silent. In fact, nowhere in the first chapter did Jonah actually call out to God. Had he done so, there would have been no need to throw him into the deep.

The second half of the first verse gives the reader insight as to where Jonah cried out to the Lord: "Out of the belly of Sheol I cried." In the Hebrew Bible, Sheol is the place people go after they die (Gen 37:35). People descend into Sheol (Num 16:33; 1 Kings 2:6). Sheol is found under the sea (Ezek 31:15). These descriptions of Sheol highlight the foolishness of Jonah's flight down to Joppa, down into the boat, and then down into the sea. *Down*, especially in the sea, is not the direction one wanted to go. People do not praise God in Sheol (Ps 6:5); neither do people find meaningful work, knowledge, or wisdom there (Eccl 9:10). Human beings could do nothing to escape Sheol (Job 7:9; Ps 89:48). That being said, God is present in Sheol even if people are not aware of the divine presence (Ps 139:8). Furthermore, God has the power both to take people down to Sheol and to raise them up (1 Sam 2:6; Pss 55:15; 86:13). Sometimes, psalmists use Sheol as a synonym for being near death. At the bottom of the sea, Jonah is physically near Sheol. Jonah is also near death, making him existentially near to Sheol as well. From the edge of death, Jonah cries out to the Lord, and the Lord hears the prophet's cry.

Strikingly, Jonah declares that it is God who cast him into the deep (2:3). The reader knows that the sailors laid hands on Jonah and hurled him into the sea, but Jonah realizes that the sailors played only a small part in a much larger conflict. Jonah's attempt to flee the presence of the Lord brought him into an unwinnable conflict with the God of heaven and earth. God directly blocked his journey with the wind and indirectly brought his flight to a halt through the hands of the sailors. Attributing Jonah's hurling into the sea to God's hands is akin to the psalmist's thoughts in Psalm 32. There the psalmist, refusing to repent, remains silent about his sins. He suffers the consequences of his sins and views these consequences as the hand of God "heavy on me" (Ps 32:4). For Hebrews, the consequence of one's sins could be attributed to God's desire to pressure a person toward repentance.

WATER

Water plays an evocative role in biblical literature. In Genesis 1:1-2, the deep represents the chaotic and formless nature of the earth before God's ordering work of creation. The depths remain a place of chaos and destruction throughout the Scriptures. The deep bursts forth to cover the earth during the time of Noah (Gen 7:11). In Exodus, God pushes back the deep to lead the Israelites to salvation but then buries Pharaoh's armies beneath the waters. In Micah, God casts Israel's sins into the depths of the sea (Mic 7:19). In Psalms, the deep frequently serves as a metaphor for overwhelming circumstances that threaten to undo someone (Ps 69:2, 14, 15; 88:6). Because the deep is unfathomable to human beings, it also serves as a metaphor for God's own thoughts (Ps 36:6; 42:7). To

---

Cosmic Terms

The sea and the river mentioned in Jonah 2:3 evoke ancient Near Eastern mythological images of the chaos battle in which the deity defeats Yam (sea), also called Nahar (river), who represent chaos. In the Baal myth, Baal defeats Yam but later loses to Mot (death):

And the axe leapt from the hand of Baal,
   Like an eagle from his fingers.
It struck the skull of his Highness Yam,
   Judge Nahar between the eyes.
Yam collapsed,
   He fell to the earth.
His joints quivered,
   And his pelvis shook.
Baal wanted to drag away and put Yam down,
   He wanted to finish off Nahar.

In Enuma Elish, the battle of Marduk and Tiamat pits the great god Marduk against the forces of chaos who fight with Tiamat (from which the Hebrew word for "the great deep," *tĕhôm*, derives) plays out a similar scene. Tiamat's body is split in two to keep the waters of heaven from the earth. These cosmic images play out in the Old Testament as allusions to YHWH's power over the deep and the sea. In addition to Jonah 2, one sees this language in several Psalms (e.g., 69:14-15; 77:16-18; 107:21-29) and in Hab 3:14-15.

Baal myth adapted from Johannes C. de Moor, An Anthology of Religious Texts from Ugarit (Leiden: Brill, 1987) 41.

God, however, the deep is as water in a bottle (Ps 33:7). Furthermore, the Lord has absolute control over the waters of the earth (Ps 135:6).

For Jonah, the waters finally destroy the illusion that he could resist God's call without significant consequences. Verse 4 proves difficult to translate. One textual variant, found in the Masoretic Text and followed by the NIV, reads, "yet I will look again at your holy temple." If this text is followed, Jonah's words reflect his thoughts from the belly of the fish. God has already saved him from drowning, and Jonah now trusts that he will worship in the temple again. The NRSV and others follow the Septuagint, which reads as a question: "How shall

I look again upon your holy temple?" This second choice fits the narrative better. The flood surrounds Jonah. God's waves and billows pass over him (see Ps 42:7). Jonah finally confronts the futility of his flight from God. Where can Jonah go to flee from the presence of the Lord? Nowhere. Attempts to do so lead only to destruction. In 2:4, Jonah realizes the finality of his decision to flee from God's presence by confessing that he has been driven from the very sight of God. Through a rhetorical question, he laments that he will never again view God's holy temple. A desire to flee God's presence motivated Jonah's flight in the first place, but now that the prophet is close to achieving his initial aim, the prospect of life without God terrifies him.

[handwritten margin note: LOVE WITH NO GOD]

Jonah Remembers the Lord, 2:5-7

The second section of this song reviews the existential crisis that Jonah faced but then turns its attention toward Jonah's prayer and the Lord's response. Verses 5 and 6 note that Jonah's journey away from God's call has reached its conclusion. Jonah went down to Joppa (1:3), down into the boat (1:5), and has now gone "down" to the very bottom of the sea. The weeds wrapped around Jonah's head "at the roots of the mountains" (2:5-6) are weeds at the bottom of the ocean. Jonah now finds himself both spatially and existentially at the edge of Sheol, here called "the Pit." Death is imminent. As noted above, Jews would often speak of being near death as being in the depths (Ps 107:23-32; Exod 15:5-10). Jews did not always view death as a specific moment; it was often seen as a process that could occur over an extended time. Jonah was in that process. His life was "ebbing away" (2:7). As Fretheim notes, "Jonah was . . . at the point where he was more dead than alive."[6]

As Jonah slips into death, he remembers the Lord. Remembering the Lord involves not just recollection of who God is and what God has done. Remembering also serves as one of the primary tasks of the covenant community; by remembering the Lord, Jonah takes his place, however belatedly, back in the fold of God. In remembering the Lord, Jonah offers up a prayer and likely assumes it is his last. The psalm does not convey the content of Jonah's prayer, and there is no formal admission of wrongdoing recorded. Perhaps Jonah offered a heartfelt "I'm sorry." Maybe all he could do was cry for help. Anne Lamott calls the prayer for help "The first great prayer."[7] The Psalms abound with examples of God helping those who cry out for help (Pss 18:6;

30:2; 31:22; 40:1; 121:1-2). Whatever the content of Jonah's prayer, the words reached the Lord in the temple.

The fact that Jonah lives to compose this psalm testifies to the fact that God has rescued the wayward prophet. Jonah affirms that God "brought up my life from the Pit" (2:6). Jonah knows how close he came to dying. Within the larger narrative, the psalm helps us recognize that Jonah viewed the fish as a rescue, not a punishment. Though confined, Jonah is not dead. The fact that Jonah still has breath in his lungs is reason enough to offer up this prayer of gratitude from the belly of the fish.

Jonah Makes a Vow to the Lord, 2:8-9

The tone of the song takes a turn in Jonah 2:8. This change seems dramatic to the modern reader, but it is in keeping with the conventions of thanksgiving songs that often end with a didactic word to the congregation. The poet warns that those who "worship vain idols forsake their true loyalty." There are many contexts in Israel's history in which this line would make sense. Jonah's story is not one of those. While the sailors cried out to foreign gods, they were foreigners. No one expected them to worship the Lord even though they were the first to do so in this story. Even when addressing the Ninevites, the issue will be their wickedness and not their worship. Though he has done his best to flee the one true God, nowhere does Jonah appear to worship other gods. Maybe this line appears simply as a reassertion of the Jewish belief that Yahweh was the only true God. God has acted in an unmistakable way in this story. To trust in any other god would be utter foolishness. Those gods are "worthless" (NIV). Furthermore, those who turn to false gods abandon the one God who remains loyal to them. The Hebrew word translated "true loyalty" in the NRSV and "love" in the NIV is *ḥesed*. While humans can show loyal love to one another (1 Sam 20:14), most often the word refers to God's covenantal love toward humans (Ps 100:5). Jonah's story illustrates God's undying love for human beings. God shows compassion to the sailors, the Ninevites, and even Jonah.

Jonah concludes this psalm by contrasting himself with those who abandon God for idols. "But I" sounds a bit strong coming from the one who has spent the last full chapter on the lam from God. The pagan sailors offered prayers well before Jonah did. Nevertheless, Jonah vows to praise the Lord with his voice and to offer sacrifices to God in the temple. Vows are a common feature of thanksgiving songs. Likely, Jonah intends to offer the Lord a sacrifice of thanksgiving

Paying Vows

Vows in the OT represent human responses to distress that essentially bargain with God. In the Hebrew Bible, vows can take place in cultic and non-cultic contexts. In cultic vows, payment usually involved ritual sacrifice from the person who made the vow, and the payment was seen as a kind of repayment for life. Consequently, the amount of the vow was determined by the status of the individual, as illustrated in the following text:

> Speak to the people of Israel and say to them: When a person makes an explicit vow to the Lord concerning the equivalent for a human being, the equivalent for a male shall be: from twenty to sixty years of age the equivalent shall be fifty shekels of silver by the sanctuary shekel. If the person is a female, the equivalent is thirty shekels. If the age is from five to twenty years of age, the equivalent is twenty shekels for a male and ten shekels for a female. If the age is from one month to five years, the equivalent for a male is five shekels of silver, and for a female the equivalent is three shekels of silver. And if the person is sixty years old or over, then the equivalent for a male is fifteen shekels, and for a female ten shekels. If any cannot afford the equivalent, they shall be brought before the priest and the priest shall assess them; the priest shall assess them according to what each one making a vow can afford. (Lev 27:2-8)

The payment for vows of a woman could also be nullified by fathers or husbands if they stated their disapproval upon hearing the vow (Num 30:3-15).

Non-cultic vows often take place in battles (e.g, Num 21:1-3), under personal duress (e.g., Gen 28:20-22; see 31:11-13; 35:1-3), or in response to answered prayer (e.g., Absalom's statement of the need to repay a vow in 2 Sam 15:7-8, even though Absalom uses this vow as a ruse to begin his rebellion against David).

once he returns safely to Jerusalem (Lev 7:11-18; Pss 50:14; 107:22; 116:17). Jonah's promise is reminiscent of a foxhole conversion; his vows may be an attempt to ensure that God follows through with this miraculous deliverance via fish.

The final phrase of the psalm captures the theme of the entire book: "Deliverance belongs to the Lord." God chooses when and whom to deliver. No one else can prevent or manipulate God's liberating hand. Jonah acknowledges that not even the deep is too deep to prevent God from rescuing those in need. The irony in Jonah's declaration is that Jonah had attempted to prevent God from delivering the Ninevites. If the deep cannot derail God's redeeming work, neither can a peevish prophet.

The phrase is only two words in the Hebrew, *yeshuata leyahweh*. The word for deliverance shows up on the lips of the angel in Matthew 1:21. He tells Mary that she will have a son, and his name will be *Yeshua* (Jesus), for he will deliver the people from their sins. Jesus, unlike Jonah, will gladly announce the salvation of all people. Jonah, on the other hand, will go to Nineveh only belatedly. And even then, the prophet will announce God's word begrudgingly.

The Fish Vomits Jonah on Dry Land, 2:10

Jonah 2:10 moves back to prose from poetry, shifting the focus of the story from the inside of the fish back to the outside world. God has heard Jonah's prayer. The Lord, who had appointed the fish to swallow Jonah, now speaks to the fish, which responds by spewing or vomiting Jonah out on dry land. The image of the fish vomiting the prophet onto the shore is purposefully humorous. Benjamin Franklin once wrote that "Guests, like fish, stink after three days." Perhaps Jonah, a guest inside a fish, had reached the limits of his visit as well. Furthermore, the violent vomiting of Jonah proves a little cartoonish. Jonah 3:4 indicates that Jonah reached Nineveh with a day's walk, but the Assyrian city is more than three hundred miles from the Mediterranean. The fish's spewing of Jonah, then, involves a bit of exaggeration or some miraculous projectile vomiting.

TEACHING THIS CHAPTER

The second chapter of Jonah presents the reader with several key themes. First, Jonah's flight from God and subsequent sinking illustrate the fact that disobedience leads to death. Second, the consequences of our disobedience may serve as warning signs that point us back to God. Most important, this chapter affirms the great truth of the Scriptures: God will answer our cries for help. Still, when God's help arrives, it may first appear like a threat.

Sin Leads to Death

One of the consistent themes of the Scriptures is that disobedience leads to death. Moses' parting words to the Israelites in Deuteronomy 30:11-20 are to plead with them to choose life through obedience to God's commandments. He warns that the disobedient perish. Paul famously wrote, "For the wages of sin is death" (Rom 6:23). Most instructive for Jonah's case is Proverbs 14:12: "There is a way that seems right to a person, but its end is the way to death." Jonah disobeys God because he disagrees with God's potential plan to show mercy toward Nineveh (Jonah 4:2). As ridiculous as it sounds, Jonah believes that he knows better than God. It will take nearly drowning to awake Jonah from his delusions.

The words of Jonah in this chapter richly convey the trouble that any of us can find ourselves in when we depart from God's ways. When our supposed wisdom fails us, the consequences of our decisions eventually begin to pile up and threaten to overwhelm us. Broken relationships, shattered plans, legal troubles, and even physical suffering can all result from going our own way. As these consequences grow in significance, we can feel as if the waters of life are closing in, as if we are sinking deep in sin beyond the possibility of rescue. Eventually, we can even reach the point that Jonah reached and fear that we have been excluded from God's very presence.

Not everyone who sins must face the consequences of their sins as quickly as Jonah did. Some people ride the boat to Tarshish much further before encountering a storm. The consistent message of Scripture is that for those who persist in going their own way, the storm will come. God goes to great lengths to draw us back into a right relationship with the divine. Still, God will not force a person's faith. God will begrudgingly let us go our own way even if it leads to our demise. In *The Great Divorce,* his imaginative take on hell, C. S. Lewis explains, "There are only two kinds of people in the end: those who say to God, 'Thy will be done,' and those to whom God says, in the end, 'Thy will be done.' All that are in Hell, choose it."[8] Paul writes something similar in his letter to the Romans (1:28-32). When people fail to acknowledge God, God eventually gives them over to that which they desire, a life without the Lord. While people think life without God is exactly what they want, they discover, sometimes too late, that such a life leads to wickedness, malice, and hate. When we chart our own course, it leads to death.

The teacher may use Jonah's story as a way of helping members of the class think through how a life of disobedience leads to death. The class can explore this truth on an individual or a corporate level. While it is true that our individual sins lead to death, churches and families and entire societies can make decisions that lead to their own demise. Using the rising waters of Jonah 2:4 as a metaphor, the class might explore what signs we have that our lives collectively or individually are about to go under.

Warning Signs

Many people view the consequences of sin as evidence that God is eager to punish sinners. In this passage, Jonah says it is God who cast him into the deep (2:3). I am tempted when I read such words to think of students who blame their instructors for giving them a failing grade. I hear the voices of educators to their failing students: "I did not *give* you an F. You *earned* it." Responsibility for Jonah's troubles rests solely with the prophet. That does not mean others did not play a role. The sailors tossed Jonah into the deep—but only as a last resort. Is it fair for Jonah to blame God for his flight into the waters? The reader never hears directly from God that Jonah had to be tossed into the sea. This message comes through Jonah's own words (1:12). God may have given Jonah other options, but Jonah chose the sea over repentance.

Still, theologically, we can say God tossed Jonah into the sea if we insist that God made this the only option other than repentance. Even if that is so, God tosses Jonah into the waters not to punish him but to wake him up. God has been trying to get Jonah's attention since Jonah first took flight. First, God sent the storm. Then, God sent the sailors who confronted Jonah in his sin. When neither of those attempts worked, God resorted to dunking Jonah in the sea. These were not attempts to destroy Jonah; instead, God was little by little allowing Jonah to get a glimpse of where his path was leading in an effort to help Jonah wise up and turn around.

God allows us to experience the consequences of our sins, often in measured doses, as a way of awakening us to the danger of disobedience. Remember, it was only in the pigpen that the prodigal son finally came to his senses. We do not end up in the pigsty or the bottom of the sea without warning signs. When we insist on our own way, cracks quickly begin to appear in our relationships. Trouble brews in our souls. The works of the flesh displace the fruit of the Spirit (Gal 5:16-26). We can view these signs as punishments or as gracious warnings that we are on the wrong track. I remember a time when I happened to be traveling behind a friend whose car caught on fire while he was driving it. Fortunately, no one was hurt. Later, the driver admitted that his check engine light had been on for months but that he thought it was no big deal.

People often show up in the pastor's office only after the car has caught fire. A man has cheated on his wife. A woman has stolen from her workplace. They come clean about their misdeeds and then lament the warning signs they failed to heed. Often they confess, "Pastor, I am at rock bottom." Like Jonah, they feel as if they have sunk as low as a person can go. Unlike Jonah, they are not literally at the bottom of the sea. I have learned from painful experience that they've only reached rock bottom if, like Jonah, they call out to God for help. If they repent and turn to God, their circumstances may prove to be as low as they ever go. Unfortunately, if they persist in going their own way, even this dreadful spot will prove to be one more giant warning sign they failed to heed on their way to the bottom.

Our physical bodies provide excellent examples of how consequences of our actions warn of even worse consequences ahead unless we change our ways. Gaining a little weight may be a consequence of overeating and a warning sign that our eating habits need to change. High blood pressure may be a consequence of unchecked stress and a warning that we are taking on too much. Muscle pain may be a consequence of pushing ourselves beyond our limits and a warning to take life a little slower. A teacher could propose this line of thought as a way of exploring how certain troubles may be both a result of spiritual disobedience and a warning sign from God to repent.

God Rescues Those Who Call Out for Help

The psalm in Jonah 2:2-9 so evocatively conveys the consequences of sin that one might be tempted to think the main point of the song is about the results of disobedience. Instead, this psalm primarily testifies to the saving grace of God. Jonah called out to God, and God rescued him from the deep. This psalm is the song of a person redeemed from death's door. When life overwhelms us, God hears and responds to our cries for help. God's help even comes to those who suffer as a result of their own sins. In the passage from *The Great Divorce* noted above, Lewis completes his thought by continuing, "No soul that seriously and constantly desires joy will ever miss it. Those who seek find. To those who knock, it is opened."9 God will let us go our own way, even if it leads to our destruction. God does not give up on us as we go. Even as we depart from the Lord, our God remains poised to rescue us from our sins the moment we call out to God for help.

Some people remain critical of the sincerity of Jonah's repentance in light of his continued stubbornness in chapter 4. Jonah's continued struggle to fully embrace the ways of God only highlights the depth of God's grace. God does not demand pure motives before God intervenes. Nor does God ask for elaborate confessions. How elaborate could a prayer be at the bottom of the sea? My guess is that Jonah did well to get out one garbled "*Help!*" Fortunately, that was enough to spur the God of compassion to action.

God's readiness to forgive shows up powerfully in Jesus' story of the prodigal son. In commenting on this story, Philip Yancey notes that Jesus spent very little time parsing the son's motives. The son does not return out of love for the father, and he shows little remorse over the hurt he has caused. Instead, he simply grows tired of the consequences of his sin—yet all the son has to do is show up on the horizon and the father runs to embrace him. Yancey concludes, "Apparently, it matters little to God whether we approach him out of desperation or out of longing."[10] To put it another way, God does not care *why* we call for help, but *that* we call.

The basic Christian testimony is one of rescue. Classes may explore this theme in the text by sharing the ways God has rescued them from sin. While no one should be forced to share, classes may be surprised to learn of the great varieties of salvation God has brought about in the lives of church members. God rescues us from addiction, from broken relationships, from financial ruin, and, yes, from sin. Classes can also explore how difficult it is to ask for help and the freedom that occurs when we do.

What Looks Like a Threat May Be Our Deliverance

A final theme that may be explored in class discussion involves the fact that God's salvation can sometimes first appear as a threat. No sane person would describe being swallowed by a fish as a good thing, yet the fish proved to be salvation for Jonah. I do not know anyone who has been swallowed by a fish, but I do know plenty of people who came to see an overwhelming threat as a form of salvation. When a church member lost his job, he saw it as a threat. A year later, the man confessed that his firing was the best thing that had happened to him. Only in losing his job did he discover the ways his job had become an idol in his life. Only in losing his job did he discover the damage his addiction to work was doing to his family and himself. Only in losing his job was he forced to find a different job that helped him bring better balance to his life. At first, losing his job was a threatening fish. Only in being swallowed by that fish was the man saved. We could say the same for any number of threats. The class may discuss times when potential threats proved salvific.

QUESTIONS FOR REFLECTION AND DISCUSSION

1. It took reaching rock bottom before Jonah called out to God for deliverance. At what other points in the journey could Jonah have repented and turned to God? Why do we sometimes resist turning to God until it is almost too late?

2. Jonah's sins led to his literal swamping. Think of a time that your sin led to being overwhelmed. What were the warning signs that you were on a path toward destruction? What helped you finally turn back to God?

3. How might Jonah's story apply to the corporate life of the church? What signs might exist in a church's life that could warn the congregation of corporate disobedience to God's ways?

4. Jonah cried out to God, and God answered his cry. Reflect on a time when you cried out to God for help. How did God respond? Is there something in your life you need help with today? How might you cry out to God for help in this situation?

5. What does it mean for deliverance to belong to the Lord? How do we sometimes resist God's deliverance in our lives? How do we resist God's deliverance in the lives of others?

SUGGESTIONS FOR WORSHIP AND PREACHING

Order of Worship

Call to Worship based on Psalm 69:1-2
Gracious Lord, at times we gather to praise you in celebration.
For the good things you have done.
Other times we gather in desperation.
We cry out for your help.
Save us, O Lord,
For the water is up to our necks.
We are weary, and our eyes grow dim.
Yet, we wait for you.

"Love Lifted Me"

"He Is Able to Deliver Thee"

Season of Silent Prayer: In this season of prayer, call out to God to bring help to you in your area of greatest need. If you can think of no personal needs, lift up the needs of another.

"Lord, I Need You" (Christy Nockels et al., Six Steps, 2011)

"Always" (Jason Ingram and Kristian Stanfill, Six Steps, 2011)

Scripture Reading: Jonah 1:17–2:10

Choral Anthem: "Jonah" (Rollo Dilworth, Hal Leonard Co., 2004)

Sermon: The View from Rock Bottom

Hymn of Response: "Jesus, What a Friend of Sinners"

Benediction: May the God of all grace, who has called you to his eternal glory in Christ, restore, support, strengthen, and establish you. To him be the power forever and ever. Amen. (from 1 Pet 5:10-11)

Example Sermon Outline: The View of Rock Bottom

Introduction

One of my favorite things about flying involves the views from the clouds that you simply cannot get from the ground. When I fly into our small city, I can see almost the entire town at once. The bird's-eye view provides a whole new perspective on the place we call home. When viewed from the sky, buildings that seem far apart on the ground thanks to winding roads prove to be more closely connected than I realized. Neighborhoods that feel removed from one another in day-to-day life appear more clearly a part of the whole when viewed from above. Often, changes in perspective help us see familiar things in a new light. What is true for the view from above also holds for the view from below. In our text today, Jonah has a view from below. It is not just any view from below, however; Jonah has a view from the rock bottom of life.

Transition

When we left Jonah in chapter 1, he was sinking into the depths of the sea. He ended up there thanks to his own stubborn refusal to go God's way. God called Jonah to go to Nineveh to preach against the city, but Jonah refused, in part because he thought God might show grace to the wicked people there. Jonah wanted no part of that plan. So he ran. While God let him run, God did not leave Jonah alone. God first sent the storm as a way of correcting Jonah's course. When that did not work, God used the thoughtfulness of pagan sailors to prod Jonah toward faithfulness. Still, Jonah refused. When it became clear that Jonah must choose between obedience or death, Jonah chose death and had the sailors toss him into the sea.

We learn from chapter 2 that Jonah did not drown, but he almost did. In fact, he sank all the way to the bottom of the sea. According to his own testimony, the waters closed over him, the deep surrounded him, and the weeds wrapped around his head at the roots of the mountain. Where do you find the roots of the mountains? You find them at the bottom of the sea. As you remember from chapter 1, God had called Jonah to arise and go up to Nineveh. Instead, Jonah had gone down to Joppa, down into the boat, and had now completed that journey down to the bottom of the ocean. Close to death, Jonah was literally at the rock bottom of the sea and figuratively at the rock bottom of life. Jonah was as low as a soul could go. What did Jonah discover when he hit rock bottom? Jonah discovered a better perspective.

The Foolishness of Going One's Own Way

At the bottom of the sea, Jonah finally discovered what the teacher of Proverbs taught: "Sometimes there is a way that seems to be right, but in the end it is the way to death" (Prov 16:25). Jonah thought he knew better than God. Jonah thought he knew what was best for himself: do not go to Nineveh. He also thought he knew what was best for God's world: do not show mercy to the Ninevites. At the heart of all our sinning is this basic thought: "God does not know best. *I* do." God says "Nineveh," and we head to Tarshish. Some of us get further down the road than others, but eventually we all stumble and fall. Our way is not the way to freedom but instead leads us ever deeper into sin. How deep we sink depends in part on how willing we are to pay attention to God's warning signs along the way. Jonah could have turned around at the first sign of the storm. He could have reversed course after the sailors interrogated him, but he would not yield. Jonah, as we often say, would have to learn the hard way.

Many of us have to learn the hard way. A recent survey confirms that at least ten percent of us drive a car whose check engine has been on for over three months. The survey found all sorts of excuses for ignoring the light: Some people ignored the warning light because the car seemed to be running fine. Others lacked money to address the problem. Still others claimed simply not to have time to worry about getting diagnostics done and subsequent repairs. For many of these folks, the car will have to stop running before they are willing to admit there is a problem.

For Jonah, it took the very real threat of death to awaken him to his own waywardness. In this song, Jonah admits that his life is ebbing away. He is dying. It is not simply dying that jolts his conscience to awaken. Instead, it is the prospect of a life without God. Jonah had fled to Tarshish in order to get away from the Lord's presence, but now the prospect of living without God terrifies him. It takes the view from rock bottom for Jonah to figure that out.

God Alone Is Our Salvation

At rock bottom, we lose the illusion that our way is wise. We might call this realization "disillusionment." Barbara Brown Taylor points out,

> Disillusionment is not so bad. Disillusionment is the loss of illusion—about ourselves, about the world, about God—and while it is almost always painful, it is not a bad thing to lose the lies we have mistaken for the truth . . . . Disillusioned, we find out what is not true and are set free to seek what is—if we dare.[11]

At the rock bottom of the sea, Jonah lost the illusion that his way was better than God's. He also lost the illusion that he could live without God.

With his very last thoughts, Jonah remembered the Lord. With his very last breath, he called out to his God. It is not easy to call out for help, especially when doing so highlights our own inadequacies. I once built a shed of my own design for the backyard. I was proud of my shed. When people came over to visit, I would even ask them if they wanted to see my handiwork. Then one day, when I was getting a rake out of my shed, I became less proud of my efforts. The west Texas wind blew the door shut, and I immediately recognized a design flaw: I had not made a way to open the shed from the inside. I was locked inside my own shed.

If not for the fact that my two-year-old son was asleep in the house, I simply would have waited in the shed until my wife, who was out running errands, returned and started to look for me. Realizing my son might awake at any moment, I mustered up the courage to call out loudly for help. Actually, at first, my cry was not loud. I almost did not want anyone to find me. It is humiliating to have to cry aloud for help. For some of us, we have to be trapped in the sea, or trapped in our shed, before we do. Only when Jonah was at rock bottom did he finally cry out for help. In fact, his prayer from the bottom of the sea is the first word that Jonah speaks to God in this entire situation.

An Astounding View of God's Love

The remarkable thing about this story is not that it took reaching rock bottom before Jonah was motivated to cry for help. That story is as common as our humanity. The remarkable part of this story is the length God will go to rescue wayward children. Pitiful Jonah offers up the smallest of cries at the very last moment of his life, and God responds. The text reports that God appointed a fish to come and swallow Jonah (Jonah 1:17). After Jonah spends three days and three nights inside the fish, the Lord speaks to the fish, which then vomits Jonah up onto the shore.

People have wasted a lot of energy trying to figure out if a person could actually be swallowed by a fish. Some argue that the story is a parable. Others take it as fact. Either way, the prospect of a man being rescued from the deep by a fish is patently absurd, and that absurdity is the point of the story. God will go to absurd lengths to rescue us from our sins. God will send a fish to rescue a petulant prophet. God will even send a petulant prophet to rescue a wicked city. Sometimes it takes the view from rock bottom for us to see how much God loves us.

NOTES

1. Terence E. Fretheim, *The Message of Jonah* (Minneapolis: Augsburg, 1977) 97.

2. Charles R. Brown, "What Jonah Did," *The Gospel for Main Street* (New York: Century, 1930) 89–101; reprinted in *20 Centuries of Great Preaching*, vol. 7, ed. Clyde E. Fant, Jr. and William Pinson, Jr. (Waco: Word, 1971) 206–207.

3. Fretheim, *The Message of Jonah*, 95.

4. James L. Mays, *Psalms*, Interpretation (Louisville KY: John Knox, 1994) 24.

5. Aldous Huxley, "Jonah," *The Cherry Tree: A Collection of Poems*, ed. G. Grigson (New York: Vanguard, 1959) 211.

6. Fretheim, *The Message of Jonah*, 99.

7. Anne Lamott, *Help, Thanks, Wow: Three Essential Prayers* (New York: Penguin, 2012) 14.

8. C. S. Lewis, *The Great Divorce* (New York: Touchstone, 1974) 72.

9. Ibid.

10. Philip Yancey, *Soul Survivor* (New York: Doubleday, 2001) 44.

11. Barbara Brown Taylor, *The Preaching Life* (Cambridge MA: Cowley, 1993) 8.

JONAH PREACHES AND NINEVEH REPENTS

Jonah 3:1-10

Chapter 3 begins and ends with second chances. First, God re-commissions Jonah to go and preach the word of the Lord to the Ninevites. When the Ninevites hear the message and repent, God grants this wicked city a second chance as well. Between this pair of second chances, the humor of the story continues. Jonah preaches one of the poorest sermons in the Bible and converts the whole city with it. The Ninevites repent so wholeheartedly that even their animals participate in the process. Amid the humor, the reader gets a running glimpse of God's strong desire to forgive sins. The reader also learns of God's desire to include both reluctant insiders and ignorant outsiders in God's divine plans.

A SECOND COMMISSIONING, 3:1-3

In Jonah 3:1-2, the word of the Lord comes again to Jonah. Lest there be any confusion, the text makes plain that this is the second time this has happened. The Lord graciously grants Jonah a second chance. There are a few key differences in this second commissioning. The prophet is identified only by his name, not by his parentage. By now, the reader knows who Jonah is as much by his character as by his familial background. Again, the Lord calls Jonah to get up and go to Nineveh, the great city. This time, instead of preaching against the city, as in Jonah 1:2, the Lord instructs Jonah to proclaim the message that the Lord will give him. Does this indicate that God's message has changed? The reader does not know for sure. All we know of this message will be what we learn from Jonah's sermon in 3:4.

The most significant difference in chapter 3 involves the prophet. Jonah's response to God's second commission differs radically from his response to the first. In chapter 1, God told Jonah to "Go at once to Nineveh," and Jonah fled in the other direction. Here, Jonah sets out and goes to Nineveh. In the first chapter, Jonah fled the presence of the Lord. Now, Jonah travels "according to the word of the LORD" (3:3).

Before plunging into the heart of Jonah's interaction with the Ninevites, the narrator pauses to remind the reader about the change of setting. Jonah is in Nineveh, "an exceedingly large city" (3:3). All along, the narrator has described Nineveh as a large city. Now, the author elaborates on that description. Nineveh is so large that it requires three days to traverse. Archaeological evidence suggests that the narrator exaggerates since, at the city's most successful period, it was only three miles across at its widest point. The city walls were less than eight miles in circumference.[1] Most scholars understand the exaggeration as an indication that Jonah was written for an audience far removed from the eighth century. Over the intervening years, Nineveh's reputation for power eclipsed its actual size. A few scholars attempt to explain the exaggeration by noting that the narrator may have both the city and its outlying areas in mind. Attempts to justify the exaggeration miss the point. The narrator describes Nineveh's size for literary and not simply historical reasons. In the text, Nineveh's size helps highlight both the enormity of the city's conversion (3:5) and the pettiness of Jonah's perspective compared to God's compassion (4:11).

JONAH PREACHES AND THE NINEVITES REPENT, 3:4-5

After a roller coaster of a journey, Jonah finally walks into Nineveh and begins to preach. One would think that after the events inside the fish, Jonah would take up the task the Lord has given him with gusto. Jonah does not. First, the text notes that Jonah preaches to only about a third of the city. The reader has already been informed that it takes three days to walk across Nineveh. Jonah's mission trip into the city lasts only a day. Any image the reader has of preachers adding another night to the revival services or extending the invitation for multiple verses of a hymn to coax one more believer down the aisle is in contrast to Jonah's approach. Jonah does only the bare minimum to obey the Lord's command. Go and preach to Nineveh? Jonah does, but just barely.

As short as Jonah's preaching tour is, the length of his journey far exceeds the length of his sermon. Measuring just five words in the Hebrew, Jonah's homily is one of the shortest in the entire Bible. Furthermore, the sermon fails to communicate anything but the most basic information: "Forty days more, and Nineveh shall be overthrown." Jonah provides no reasons for this message of doom. Neither does he inform the Ninevites of a possible remedy, even though Jonah's conversation with God will reveal that the prophet knew a remedy was possible (4:2). While it is possible that this short sentence summarizes a longer message, the point still holds. Jonah did as little as possible to meet the requirements of God's call on his life.

The few words Jonah uses lack any precision. While forty days is a favorite time frame for biblical authors (Gen 7:4; Exod 24:18; Num 13:25), Jonah's use of the phrase is imprecise. At first reading, his sermon makes it sound like God will destroy Nineveh at the end of forty days, but the Hebrew could also mean that God will punish Nineveh within the next forty days.[2] Jonah's language does not make it clear. Exactly what will happen to Nineveh at the end of that period proves equally ambiguous. The verb that Jonah uses can be translated "to overturn." The same word is sometimes translated "to turn around" or "to transform."[3] This ambiguity allows the sermon to be true with a variety of results. If God destroys Nineveh, the city will be overturned like ancient Sodom and Gomorrah (Gen 19:25, 29). If they repent, the city will be turned around for good. Jonah clearly hopes for the former and not the latter. The purpose of Jonah's poorly communicated sermon may be to increase the chances that God will destroy Nineveh. Either Jonah's words will confuse the Ninevites so that they take no course of action, or they will offend them so that they react defensively and take the wrong actions. Either way, Jonah does not want his preaching to lead to the Ninevites' repentance.

While Jonah does everything in his power to prevent the Ninevites from responding positively to his message, they do so nonetheless. In fact, their repentance is both citywide and wholehearted. Like a wildfire spreading through their city, word somehow spreads from those who heard Jonah's sermon in the first third of the city to those who had not. All the people believe God. The narrator's word choice is notably different here in chapter 3. Whereas the sailors feared God, the Ninevites believe God. The Hebrew conveys the idea of trust or reliance.[4] In the Bible, trust in God leads to righteousness. The best example comes from the life of Abraham. We learn from Genesis 15:6 that Abraham "Believed the LORD; and the LORD reckoned it to him as righteousness."

It is notable that the word for God here is "Elohim" and not "Yahweh." In fact, throughout the narrative, the Ninevites use this more generic name for God (3:5, 8, 9, and 10). Their use of this word may reflect their status as outsiders. It may also reflect the fact that Jonah did not adequately identify the God who was upset with them. Despite the fact that they have only the most basic information, the Ninevites, like the sailors, do not hesitate to seek to appease whatever God may be upset with them. They acknowledge both their own sinfulness and the fact that only God can save them.

The Ninevites' belief finds concrete expression in the proclamation of a fast and the wearing of sackcloth. By the time of Jesus, fasting played an important role in Jewish life. Pharisees fasted several times a week. In much of the Hebrew Scriptures, fasting is less regular. Far from being a routine part of one's spiritual practices, fasting served to mark an unusual moment in an individual or community's life. David fasted as a way of pleading for the life of his child (2 Sam 12:16). Nehemiah fasted as a sign of his grief over the dilapidated state of Jerusalem (Neh 1:4). Communities fasted as a way of mourning leaders (2 Sam 1:12). Ezra proclaimed a fast in order to seek God's protection over a journey (Ezra 8:21). The people of Israel fasted and wore sackcloth under Nehemiah's leadership as a sign of corporate confession (Neh 9:1). Here, the Ninevites fast as a sign of repentance.

Sackcloth

 Sackcloth was a piece of clothing to be worn in times of general sorrow (1 Kgs 20:31-32), individual mourning (Gen 37:34), communal mourning (2 Sam 3:31), or repentance (Lam 2:10; Joel 1:8; Esth 4:1-3). Because it was usually made of goat's hair, sackcloth was generally black. People wore it as an outer garment, sometimes specifically over the loins (Amos 8:10).

The Ninevites' response includes everyone from the least to the greatest. The entire community repents of their sins. The Ninevites do all of this despite the fact that Jonah has provided them with no instructions on what to do. His sermon was without application. Somewhat miraculously, they have intuitively reacted to Jonah's sermon in the same way that repentant Jews would have reacted. In fact, their wholesale repentance exceeds almost every other communal response to God in all of the Scriptures. No one reportedly complains. No one objects. All return to God despite Jonah's poor efforts in reaching them with the good news of God.

For some scholars, Nineveh's wholesale conversion supports the idea that this story is fiction. They note that it is unlikely that a city hostile to Israel and Israel's God would so completely and wholeheartedly respond to a Jewish prophet's sermon. While the Assyrians kept significant records of what happened in their kingdom, no record exists that corroborates the account in the book of Jonah. Fretheim argues that Nineveh's conversion is one more example of the narrator's attempts to push this story to absurd lengths. The radical nature of the Ninevites' conversion reemphasizes the main themes of the book, including "the potential effect that the preaching of the Word of God has" and the "difficulty that God has had with his own people."[5] Other scholars insist that the conversion of a whole city is not as far-fetched as it sounds. Stuart maintains that troubles in Assyria, including famine, pestilence, internal corruption, and military decline, may have made the city ripe for religious revival.[6] Within the context of the story, the Ninevites' radical repentance serves to highlight the power of the proclaimed word of God. If these are the results a reluctantly preached sermon gets, how might people respond to a prophet of the Lord who is dedicated to his task?

The King of Nineveh Catches Up to His Kingdom, 3:6-9

In keeping with the narrator's propensity for turning convention on its head, the king of Nineveh does not lead his people into repentance but follows them there. To give the king credit, he follows them with gusto. The text reports that the arrival of news spurs the king to action. It is unclear if the news he receives includes only Jonah's sermon or also the people's response. Either way, the king does his best to catch up with his people's reaction to Jonah's message. The king rises from his throne, takes off his royal clothes, puts on sackcloth, and sits in ashes (3:6). Each of these steps serves as a profound symbol of humility for one whose position rarely requires such acts.

Whether from his own extreme sense of shame or from an attempt to get out in front of his people once again, the king ups the ante by expanding the fast the people had proclaimed. On their own, the people had proclaimed a fast from the least to the greatest. The king now issues a royal decree extending that fast and the wearing of sackcloth to the animals of the kingdom. Furthermore, not only will the entire kingdom refuse to eat, but the king also commands that they shall refrain from drinking water. Instead, they will all, great and small, human beings and animals, "cry mightily to God" (3:8). The image of a cow dressed in sackcloth, bleating out penitent cries, strikes the modern reader as humorous; perhaps the narrator means for it to be so. The image does highlight the complete seriousness with which the Ninevites seek the Lord's forgiveness after hearing Jonah's message.

Isaiah 58:5-7

Is such the fast that I choose,
a day to humble oneself?
Is it to bow down the head like a bulrush,
and to lie in sackcloth and ashes?
Will you call this a fast,
a day acceptable to the Lord?
Is not this the fast that I choose:
to loose the bonds of injustice,
to undo the thongs of the yoke,
to let the oppressed go free,
and to break every yoke?
Is it not to share your bread with the hungry,
and bring the homeless poor into your house;
when you see the naked, to cover them,
and not to hide yourself from your own kin?

Most important, the king's decree calls on every person to "turn from their evil ways and from the violence that is in their hands" (3:8). The Hebrew prophets repeatedly assert that fasting, without an accompanying change in behavior, does little to sway the Lord's mind. King Jehoiakim once proclaimed a fast for Judah, but then he rejected the message of the Lord, going so far as to burn the scroll delivered to him by Jeremiah's servant Baruch (Jer 36). Needless to say, Jehoiakim's fast proved ineffective in arousing the mercy of God. The prophet Isaiah explicitly condemns fasts that are void of ethical concerns. The king of Nineveh likely does not have access to the prophet's teaching. Nevertheless, he instinctively knows that true repentance requires signs of contrition and acts of obedience.

If the king's theological insight into the true nature of repentance appears unusually perceptive for a pagan king, his understanding of God's freedom to respond is equally astonishing. The king understands that he cannot manipulate God into action. The Ninevites' actions do not guarantee a gracious response from the Lord. The king motivates the people to action with the humblest of acknowledgments: "Who knows? God may relent and change his mind" (3:9). The king's words echo the words of the captain of the ship in Jonah 1:6. They also sound remarkably similar to the prophet Joel, who likewise calls the people to a fast in the hopes that God will relent from sending destruction:

Yet even now, says the LORD,
return to me with all your heart,

with fasting, with weeping, and with mourning;
rend your hearts and not your clothing.
Return to the LORD, your God,
for he is gracious and merciful,
slow to anger, and abounding in steadfast love,
and relents from punishing.
Who knows whether he will not turn and relent,
and leave a blessing behind him. (Joel 2:12-14a)

The king understands that the Ninevites cannot force God's hand. They can repent. They can call out for mercy. They can hope that the Lord will respond.

This pagan king understands what Israel would often forget. God is under no obligation to show mercy to human beings. Again and again, God has proven to be merciful, but human beings are in no position to presume upon that mercy. Jeremiah had to warn the people of Judah that the temple of the Lord did not guarantee military victory (Jer 7:4). The people could not continue in their sins and assume that God would simply be merciful. God is merciful, but unchecked sin leads to destruction. A person who presumes upon God's mercy misunderstands the nature of our relationship with God. God is not a magical force that can be manipulated into doing our bidding. God is the sovereign Lord who may show us mercy, but is also under no obligation to do so. Remarkably, the king of Nineveh understands this truth whereas many in Israel's history did not.

GOD SHOWS MERCY TO NINEVEH, 3:10

When God sees how the Ninevites "turned from their evil ways," God turns from sending evil on the Ninevites. God's turning is explained bluntly: "God changed his mind" (3:10). This phrase causes some consternation among modern interpreters who insist that God does not change. Nevertheless, the idea of God changing course appears several times in the Hebrew Scriptures. In Exodus 32, the Lord confronts Moses with the news of the people's worship of the golden calf (Exod 32:7-8). God clearly intends to destroy the people for this grievous sin (32:10). After Moses intercedes on behalf of the people (32:11-13), the Lord "changed his mind about the disaster that he planned to bring on his people" (32:14). In 2 Samuel 24:16, the Lord relents from destroying Jerusalem

YHWH Repenting

The idea of YHWH repenting, relenting, or changing YHWH's mind surprises many Christians who have grown up hearing language of predestination and God's immutability. Yet, the Hebrew Bible repeatedly reports that God repented concerning something God had done or was about to do. This happens at least 21 times in the Old Testament: Gen 6:6; Exod 32:12, 14; Judg 2:18; 1 Sam 15:11, 35; 2 Sam 24:16; Jer 18:8, 10; 26:3, 13, 19; 42:10; Joel 2:13, 14; Amos 7:3, 6; Jonah 3:9, 10; 4:2; 1 Chr 21:15. Several things can motivate YHWH's change of heart, including human intercession, divine compassion, and human repentance. This variety also occurs in phrases using the verb turn (*šûb*) as in Zech 1:3; Mal 3:7; Pss 6:4; 90:13. This portrayal means that the future is open for the biblical God. Over and over, whether in terms of human behavior or human pleading, God responds to the responses human beings make. To be sure, this idea of "repentance" differs from human repentance from sin. YHWH's changing YHWH's mind generally flows from YHWH's mercy overcoming YHWH's wrath. YHWH's repentance is not based on sin but on compassion.

over David's sin. In Amos 7, God again relents from plans to destroy Israel as a punishment for its transgressions. In each case where God relents from bringing evil on God's people, God exemplifies the fact that Israel's God is "merciful and gracious, slow to anger, and abounding in steadfast love and faithfulness" (Exod 34:6).

These examples from Israel's history provide a framework for understanding how God changed course with Israel on several occasions. These examples do not, however, prepare the reader for God's actions toward Nineveh. In each case with Israel, God acts out of covenantal loyalty to Israel. In fact, Moses appeals to covenantal loyalty when he speaks on the people's behalf. But God has no covenant with Nineveh. Why does God relent from sending punishment on them? Jeremiah provides some insight into this discussion when he describes the Lord as a potter. Just as a potter may make or destroy a vessel in his hand, so too may God rescue or destroy a country according to divine purposes. The image of a vessel in the potter's hand applies to Israel. It also applies to other nations. According to Jeremiah, the Lord declares, "At one moment I may declare concerning a nation or a kingdom, that I will pluck up and break down and destroy it, but if that nation, concerning which I have spoken, turns from its evil, I will change my mind about the disaster I intend to bring on it" (Jer 18:7-8). Nineveh illustrates Jeremiah's point. God can do as God pleases. God can even show grace to outsiders.

While no one should presume upon God's grace, neither should a person be surprised that God shows mercy to the Ninevites. Jonah is not surprised by God's actions, even if God's mercy angers him (4:2). That God shows mercy to all the peoples of the earth and not simply to those who claim to be God's people proves to be one of the main themes of this text. That the Ninevites prove incredibly responsive to Jonah's preaching anticipates the wholehearted response Gentiles will show to the apostles' preaching.

TEACHING THIS CHAPTER

The third chapter of Jonah provides resolution to one of the lingering questions in this book: "What will happen to Nineveh?" Once Jonah preaches, the Ninevites repent, and God relents. There is notably less tension in this chapter than in the previous two. If not for Jonah's surprising response in chapter 4, a person might expect God's compassion at the end of chapter 3 to serve as the conclusion of the story. Beneath the apparent tidiness of this chapter reside several issues worth exploring. First, the story of Nineveh's repentance reaffirms the scope of God's mission in the world. Second, the story of Nineveh's repentance reveals the power of the word of God to bring about change in the lives of people. Third, repentance remains the key human response to God's actions in the world. Last, God's willingness to change course reveals the unchanging nature of God's love for the world.

The Scope of God's Compassion

In his classic text, *Transforming Mission*, David J. Bosch explains how the church's doctrine of mission finds its beginning in the very nature of God. The church engages in mission because God is already engaged in mission. We call God's mission the *misseo Dei*.[7] Recognizing that God has a mission involves understanding the fact that God is for the world. This is a part of God's own nature. God is not simply for one part of the world but is for the *whole* world. When God chooses a particular people like the church or Israel, God does so for the purpose of redeeming all of humanity. Any concept of God that does not include God's heart for the nations fails to depict the God of the Bible accurately.

The theme of God-for-the-whole-world shows up throughout the New Testament (Matt 28:19-20; Mark 13:10; Luke 24:46-47; John 3:16; Rev 22:2). The theme is less prominent in the Hebrew Scriptures. Nevertheless, the idea of God blessing the nations through Israel is present in several texts. First, God assures Abraham that all the nations of the earth will be blessed through his offspring (Gen 22:18). The prophet Isaiah picks up this theme in earnest. Israel, sometimes personified as the suffering servant, will serve as a light to the nations (Isa 2:2-4; 42:1; 51:4; 56:7; 60:3). Few places in the Hebrew Scriptures prove as illustrative of God's concern for the nations as the book of Jonah. In this short book, God shows concern for a foreign nation—an incredibly wicked nation. God shows concern for this wicked nation and saves them. If God will save the Ninevites, can any nation lie beyond God's care?

While the book of Jonah provides us with a beautiful picture of God's care for the nations, it is not a manual for church missions. The story is more illustrative than instructive. The picture this short story draws is striking, and if the book was written years or even centuries after Assyria's demise, the point becomes even more compelling. Assyria's historical reputation for wickedness, violence, and evil stands on par with that of the Nazis. The narrator's insistence that God has compassion on the Assyrians stretches the idea of God's compassion as far as one can take it. As we shall see in the next chapter, this radical depiction of God's love for evildoers stretches Jonah well beyond where he would like to go. If God's compassion is for the Assyrians, then God must have compassion for all people. If we have been fortunate enough to experience God's compassion in our lives, then we, like Jonah, find ourselves called to share that compassion with others. If there are no people who fall beyond the scope of God's compassion, then neither should we place limits on the compassion we offer others.

In his commentary on the book of Jonah, James Limburg recalls a mural on the wall of a museum in Rüdesheim, Germany, that retells the story of Jonah. One sees the fish, the ship, and Jonah looking over the city waiting for God to act. When you look closely, you realize the city that Jonah overlooks is not ancient Nineveh but modern Mainz, a nearby town. Limburg comments on the change: "Nineveh is the city nearby that needs to hear the prophetic word."[8] What city's skyline might your class substitute for Nineveh in a similar mural? How can we be certain that God cares for these places in the same way God cares for us?

The Power of God's Word

Jonah's sermon to the Ninevites would earn poor marks in almost any preaching class. Nevertheless, the response to Jonah's sermon exceeds anything the world has ever seen outside of the scenes found in the first few chapters of the book of Acts. The book of Jonah affirms the power of God's word let loose in the world. Jonah's example should not be used as an excuse for poor preaching. Those called to preach the word of God should employ all their skill to this high task. Nevertheless, Jonah's example reminds us that preaching is first and foremost an act of God and not of men or women. God's word has a power that goes well beyond the rhetorical skills of the preacher.

Every preacher I know has had the experience of preaching a sermon they thought was excellent, only to have it fall flat. Those same preachers can recall a sermon they know was no good that received an outsized response. While I have never had the kind of response Jonah received, I can remember sermons that deeply moved many in my congregation even though I finished the sermon dissatisfied with my own efforts. Again and again, I rediscover the timeless truth that any power in the pulpit comes not from my own cleverness but from God's gracious willingness to show up in both the speaker's words and the listeners' ears.

How did God show up in Jonah's short sermon? God's presence likely showed up in the fact that Jonah delivered a word from God about the reality of Nineveh's predicament. In his brilliant book on preaching in a postmodern age, *The End of Words*, Richard Lischer argues, "The cure for pulpit dullness is not brilliance but reality."[9] Jonah's words failed to be elegant, but they were truthful. Nineveh's sin put the city on a path toward destruction. The truthfulness of Jonah's sermon struck a chord in the hearts of the Ninevites. Likely, the Spirit of God had already been at work in their hearts. They could see with their own eyes the devastation brought about in their community and in their families by the prevalence of violence in their land. Jonah's sermon helped them name their reality and compelled them to seek the Lord's help in altering their hopeless course.

Part of the power present in Jonah's sermon likely came from the fact that Jonah was the first to speak the truth to the Ninevites in a long time. Those of us who frequently preach or listen to sermons often expect very little. One of the reasons for our low expectations may include the sheer number of sermons we have spoken or heard. We arrive at the text and think *"We have heard this before."* As a result, our hearts remain closed to hearing a new word from God. Often, those who have never heard the gospel stories can help those of us who have been in the church a long time to hear the stories anew. For instance, one

Sunday the lesson in our collegiate class focused on the crucifixion. When the teacher finished telling the story of Jesus' death on the cross, students began packing up their things to leave. Before they could depart, an international student from Vietnam spoke up, "That is it? That is how the story ends? That is so sad. There must be more to the story!" For a moment, the class sat in stunned silence. This young man had never heard the story of Jesus' death and resurrection. The shock of Jesus' death registered in his life in a way it no longer did for the rest of the students. As the other students shared with this young man the rest of the story, they were reminded of the power of God's word to change lives.

Jonah's poor example provides classes with the opportunity to explore the many ways God's word connects with people today. How does God's word move in the world despite our limitations? How might we be better proclaimers of God's word in the world around us? How might regular interaction with those who have never heard God's word help us maintain a healthy respect for the power of God's word in our lives today?

The Proper Response to God's Word Is Repentance

God's word stands as an act of grace in the world. Jonah instinctively knows this. Why would God speak to the Ninevites at all unless God is inclined to forgive them? God need not speak to us; nevertheless, God does. When God speaks, the proper response to God's word is repentance. Repentance is at the heart of the gospel. John the Baptist preached a message of repentance (Matt 3:5-12; Luke 3:7-14). Matthew reports that Jesus consistently preached, "Repent, for the kingdom of heaven has come near" (Matt 4:17; see also Luke 5:32; 13:3; 15:10; 24:46-47). The apostles also made repentance a key aspect of their own preaching (Acts 3:19; 8:22; 17:30).

The idea of repentance, or turning toward God, has a primary place in the Hebrew Scriptures. Theologian Stanley Grenz notes that the Hebrew word for *turn* or *return* appears more than one thousand times in the Old Testament.[10] God frequently calls on Israel to *turn* from their wicked ways and to *return* to right relationship with the Lord (Isa 31:6; Jer 3:12). The people of Israel often repented of their sins. And they often did not.

Surprisingly, the Ninevites provide us with a textbook example of repentance. First, they believed God's word (3:5). That is, the Ninevites accepted what God's prophet said about them. They were wicked. The Ninevites made no excuses for their sins. They believed their sinful ways put them on a path toward destruction. They believed they would indeed be overturned (3:4) unless they turned toward God. Their belief in God manifested itself in grief over their sins. Fasting and wearing sackcloth are both signs of mourning. Second, they resolved to "turn from their evil ways and from the violence that is in their hands" (3:8). True repentance involves not only regret over our sins but also a turning from sin itself. Third, they called out to God for mercy. The Ninevites understood they could not save themselves. While they knew God was under no obligation to save them, they also knew that God was the only one who could.

The Ninevites' example provides classes with a paradigm for exploring the role of repentance in our lives today. We shall all be overturned unless we too return to God. What does repentance look like in our lives? Which aspect of repentance do we most often forget? How does the centrality of repentance to the biblical witness shape the way we worship each week? Do we spend more time critiquing the worship of the church or responding to the God we encounter there? The appropriate response to the worship service each week does not involve critiquing the rhetorical skills of the preacher or the talents of the singers. Instead, the proper response involves determining whether God has spoken and whether we will respond with trust and obedience.

God Changes and Remains Ever Faithful

The Ninevites' willingness to turn from their sins surprises any who are familiar with the atrocities of the Assyrians. The fact that God turns from a declared course of action proves even more shocking to those schooled in the concept of God's immutability. The Scriptures confirm God's unchanging nature. The psalmist praises God as one who is always the same, whose years have no end (Ps 102:26-27). James assures his readers that with God "there is no variation or shadow due to change" (Jas 1:17). In Malachi, the Lord bluntly declares, "For I the LORD do not change" (Mal 3:6). Many take these verses, and others like them, to mean that God cannot, as the text reports, "change his mind" (3:10).

Those who wish to insist God cannot change course argue that Jonah's sermon in 3:4 really means that Nineveh would be transformed within forty days. The Hebrew for "overturned" can indeed have that meaning. Of course, positive transformation of the city does not appear to be the plain meaning of Jonah's message. The Ninevites certainly did not hear it in that way. Nor does the more positive interpretation of Jonah's sermon jibe with the plain meaning of 3:10. There, very clearly, we are told that God "changed his mind about the calamity that he had said he would bring upon them." God had threatened to punish the Ninevites. Then God relented from doing so. The verb for change can also be translated "relent" (NIV) or even "repent" (KJV). We may struggle with the idea of God repenting, but the author of Jonah did not.

Certainly, there is tension between the various biblical descriptions of God's unchanging nature and God's own actions. How can an unchanging God change? One way to resolve this question is by revisiting what the Bible means when it describes God as unchanging. To say that God never changes is another way of saying that God is always faithful, always caring, always loving. It does not mean that God is static. The overwhelming testimony of the Scriptures is of a God who interacts with humanity. In all of these interactions, God is loving. This is how God remains the same, yet for God always to love human beings requires that God sometimes change. Theologian Kevin Vanhoozer writes, "Faithfulness sometimes requires change, not sameness."[11] Vanhoozer applies this principle to the church's activity in the world, but the principle applies to God as well. As long as God is interacting with an ever-changing world, God's faithfulness to God's purposes in the world will require change. As long as the Ninevites persisted in sin, God's unchanging love required divine opposition to that sin. When the Ninevites repented, God's unchanging love required a change of course.

The classic hymn "Great Is Thy Faithfulness" memorably declares the unchanging nature of God's faithfulness. Nevertheless, in the chorus, the song praises God for the new mercies God brings each morning. These words draw from Lamentations 3:22-23: "The steadfast love of the LORD never ceases, his mercies never come to an end; they are new every morning; great is your faithfulness." Because God's love never changes, God's mercies must be new every morning. The fact that God's mercies are new implies that God's love is applied anew to our ever-changing lives each new day. This means that while God's love is unchanging, the application of that love in our lives is always changing.

In my life, I can say with confidence that the love I have for my children is unchanging. There is nothing they can do to make me love them more or less. That does not mean the *expression* of my love remains unchanging. In fact, loving my children in an unchanging way demands new expressions of my love each new day. To express my love to them today, as adolescents, in the exact same way I expressed my love to them when they were infants would be weird and inappropriate. It would also be unloving. True love, like true faithfulness, requires change. Because God has an unchanging love for the people of this planet, God changes in response to our actions, prayers, and needs.

QUESTIONS FOR REFLECTION AND DISCUSSION

1. Jonah receives a second chance from the Lord (3:1). When did someone give you a second chance? How did you respond to that new opportunity? When have you given someone a second chance? How did they respond to that opportunity?

2. The Ninevites are in danger of being overturned by their sins unless they turn to God. In what ways do our sins overturn us? How does turning to God also turn our lives upside down?

3. The Ninevites' strong response to Jonah's sermon cannot be attributed to the skill of Jonah's preaching. Why did the Ninevites respond this way? When have you responded strongly to a sermon or Bible study? What factors contributed to your response?

4. The Ninevites' repentance involved both public signs of contrition and a commitment to change their ways. What role does public confession play in our repentance today? What can be dangerous about public displays of contrition? What can be positive about these acts?

5. God forgives the Ninevites and relents from sending calamity upon them. Why do some people resist the idea that God can alter divine plans? Do you think that God changes in response to our actions and prayers? Why or why not? How do you explain the text in light of your views concerning God's unchanging nature?

SUGGESTIONS FOR WORSHIP AND PREACHING

Order of Worship

"O Worship the King"

"All Creatures of Our God and King"

New Testament Reading: Matthew 4:12-17

Choral Anthem: "There's a Wideness in God's Mercy" (Music by Sara R. Nussel; Arrangment by Brad A. Nix, Shawnee Press, 2015)

Responsive Reading Based on James 4:6-8
God delights in showing grace.
Graciously, God opposes the proud,
For pride leads to destruction.
Graciously, God exalts the humble.
Repent, therefore, and turn toward the Lord.
Draw near to God,
And God will draw near to you.

"Come, Ye Sinners, Poor and Needy"

"Softly and Tenderly"

Sermon: Turn or Be Overturned

"Only Trust Him"

Benediction: Now to him who loves us and freed us from our sins by his blood, and made us to be a kingdom, priests serving his God and Father, to him be glory and dominion forever and ever. Amen.

Example Sermon Outline: Turn or Be Overturned

Introduction
Will Willimon tells a story from early in his ministry when he attended a funeral in a rural church in Georgia. The preacher's sermon caught Willimon off guard: "It's too late for Joe. He might have wanted to get his life together. He might have wanted to spend more time with his family. He might have wanted to do that, but he's dead now. It is too late for him, but it is not too late for you. There is still time for you. You still can decide. You are still alive. It is not too late for you. Today is the day of decision."

Willimon could not believe what he was hearing. He complained to his wife about how crass, rude, and manipulative the sermon was. His wife replied, "You are right. It was disgusting. It was insensitive. Worst of all, it was also true."[12]

Growing up, people labeled these fire and brimstone sermons "Turn or burn" sermons. Like Willimon, the people I went to church with looked down on churches that consistently preached in this way. Still, I find myself agreeing with Willimon's wife that behind the fiery rhetoric is a simple truth: unless we turn to God, we will be overturned by our sin. While there may be better ways to communicate this truth than the way the preacher does in Willimon's story, the heart of the gospel involves Christ's invitation: "Repent. Turn around, for the kingdom of God is at hand."

Jonah's Sermon: Not "Turn or Burn," Just "Burn"

If the preacher in Willimon's story preached a "Turn or burn" sermon, Jonah's sermon in Jonah 3:4 deserves only half that title: "Forty days more, and Nineveh shall be overthrown!" Jonah does not tell the Ninevites why God is angry or even which god they have offended. He only tells them that they are about to be destroyed. The word for "overthrown" is the same word used in Genesis 19:29 to describe the destruction of Sodom and Gomorrah. We will learn in the next chapter that Jonah knew God might show mercy to the Ninevites if they repented, but he did not include that in his sermon. If God instructed Jonah to preach "Turn or burn," Jonah conveniently left off the front of that message. For Jonah, the sermon was simply, "Burn!"

Jonah's sermon may be one of the worst in the entire Bible. At least the preacher in Willimon's story offered the possibility of salvation to those listening to his words. Jonah does no such thing. Equally disturbing is that Jonah appears to give the message halfheartedly. While we learn that Nineveh took three days to cross, Jonah only makes it a third of the way across before he apparently calls it quits. As a child, I can remember revival preachers stretching out invitation hymns for what seemed like an infinite number of verses, all in the hopes that one sinner would repent. Jonah does the opposite. After preaching a pathetic little sermon, he picks the shortest hymn in the hymnal for the invitation song. He sings one verse and sits down. Jonah has obeyed God's command—barely. If you've never read the story before, you might come to the conclusion that Jonah did not want the Ninevites to repent. As you'll see next week, you'd be right.

The Ninevites Respond

Most people think Jonah's survival in the belly of a fish for three days and three nights is the biggest miracle in this story. The most remarkable miracle in this story, however, actually happens in Jonah 3:5. Despite Jonah's truncated sermon, "the people of Nineveh believed God" (3:5). Not just one or two of them; revival breaks out in Nineveh. Word spreads like wildfire concerning the prophet's message. Even the two-thirds of town who did not hear Jonah speak find out what he said and put their faith in God. Later, the king of Nineveh gets in on the act, extending the people's proclaimed fast to include even the cows and chickens. Collectively, they all cry out to God, asking the Lord to have mercy on their town.

It's a humorous scene with the farm animals all decked out in sackcloth as they moo and cluck their confessions to God, but it teaches us some serious things about the nature of repentance. First, the Ninevites believe God. The word for *believe* conveys the idea of trust and faith. It is the same word used in Genesis 15:6, where we are told that Abraham "believed the Lord; and the Lord reckoned it to him as righteousness." To believe God in this context meant they believed God's word concerning their sins. They understood that they were sinners without excuse and that their sin had them on a path toward destruction. They may have come to this conclusion through the influence of God's Spirit. They also may have simply looked around. A community that excels in violence and wickedness is no place to live. When the Ninevites heard Jonah's sermon, "Forty days and you will be overturned," the Ninevites may have simply looked at their troubled community and concluded, "We are already there."

A second component of the Ninevites' act of repentance involved their firm conviction that only God could save them. Dressing in sackcloth and proclaiming a fast served as signs of both their contrition and their level of desperation. They recognized they could not fix the mess they had made. They needed divine intervention. The Ninevites do commit to turning away from "their evil ways and the violence that is in their hands" (3:9), but they know this alone will not save them. Their sin has set them on a course that will not change unless God looks upon them with compassion. The king's words in verse 9 remind us that we cannot manipulate God into action. We can, however, call out to God for mercy.

God's Delights in Giving Second Chances

Verse 10 subtly reports that God saw what the Ninevites did, how they turned from their wicked ways, and then God relented from sending calamity upon them. Just like that, the Ninevites were saved. That our sins can be forgiven is the miracle of grace. Inside the church, we speak of God's grace so frequently that we forget how radical it is. I remember sitting in my office one time with a woman who was unfamiliar with the promises of Scripture. After we had visited about the different ways her sin had marred her life and the lives of others, I shared with her the glorious promise from Colossians 1:21-22. Christ has reconciled us to God through Christ's death so that we are now holy and blameless before God. She looked up and asked with astonishment, "Is that true?" God's grace can seem too good to be true.

The greatest miracle in the book of Jonah is *not* the fact that the prophet lived for three days in the belly of the fish. The most remarkable miracle in the Bible is the fact that one of the worst cities on the planet heard the word of the Lord and was saved. The revival in Nineveh is extraordinary on three fronts. First, as we have already noted, the response of the people far exceeds the skills of the preacher. Second, the sheer size of the response is beyond anything else in the Scriptures. Not even at Pentecost did a whole city repent of their sins. Third, and perhaps most important, the wicked Ninevites repent of their sins. These are people who were as bad as they could be. They delighted in torture. Violence was a way of life. Their rapid and wholesale conversion would be equivalent to all of ISIS laying down their weapons and repenting of their sins.

Asking why the Ninevites responded to Jonah's sermon as they did may be a little like asking how a man can survive in the belly of a fish for three days. The question may be a bit beyond the purposes of this book. The book of Jonah does not worry about explaining exactly how these absurd things can happen. Instead, it uses an improbable rescue by fish and an unlikely revival as a way of pointing beyond the status quo of our lives to the outlandish, even absurd nature of God's love for the world. The book of Jonah paints with bold colors and wild brush strokes a picture of the God who loves us far beyond the lines we draw. *We* love those who love us back. *God* loves everyone without fail or limit.

Conclusion

We can trust that if God gives second chances to petulant prophets and nasty Ninevites, God will delight in giving us a second chance if we turn from our sins and turn to the Lord. Jonah's sermon may have been poorly presented. It may not have even told the whole story, but what he said is true. If we remain in our sin, our lives will sow only destruction. What he should have made clearer is this: "If we confess our sins, he who is faithful and just will forgive us our sins and cleanse us from all unrighteousness" (1 John 1:9). Gratefully, the Ninevites figured that out. I pray that we do, too.

NOTES

1. Jack M. Sasson, *Jonah*, The Anchor Bible (New York: Doubleday, 1990) 230.

2. Ibid., 234.

3. T. Desmond Alexander, "Jonah: An Introduction and Commentary," in vol. 26 of *Tyndale Old Testament Commentaries* (Downers Grove IL: IVP Academic, 1988) 132.

4. Sasson, *Jonah*, 243.

5. Terence E. Fretheim, *The Message of Jonah* (Minneapolis: Augsburg, 1977) 65.

6. Douglas Stuart, *Hosea–Jonah*, Word Biblical Commentary (Grand Rapids MI: Zondervan, 1988) 490–92.

7. David J. Bosch, *Transforming Mission: Paradigm Shifts in Theology of Mission* (Maryknoll NY: Orbis, 2002) 10.

8. James Limburg, *Jonah*, The Old Testament Library (Louisville KY: Westminster/John Knox, 1993) 78.

9. Richard Lischer, *The End of Words: The Language of Reconciliation in a Culture of Violence* (Grand Rapids MI: Eerdmans, 2008) 126.

10. Stanley Grenz, *Theology for the Community of God* (Grand Rapids MI: Eerdmans, 1994) 406.

11. Kevin J. Vanhoozer, *The Drama of Doctrine: A Canonical Linguistic Approach to Christian Theology* (Louisville KY: Westminster John Knox, 2005) 126.

12. Will Willimon, "The Writing on the Wall," in *Glimpses of Heaven* (Eugene OR: Harvest House, 2013) 127.

JONAH COMPLAINS AND GOD RESPONDS

Jonah 4:1-11

Many retellings of the Jonah story, especially in children's storybooks, end the account of Jonah and the Lord with God forgiving the Ninevites. It is easy to understand why some editors make this choice. God's act of forgiveness toward the Ninevites provides a fine conclusion to the story, especially for those who like tidy endings. God called Jonah to preach to the Ninevites, but Jonah ran. God then pursued Jonah, and Jonah repented. Jonah preached, and the Ninevites turned to God. God saw the Ninevites' contrition and relented from sending calamity upon them. All's well that ends well. The only problem is that Jonah will not leave well enough alone. Jonah, who once reacted joyfully to God's mercy in his life (2:2-9), now reacts bitterly to the fact that the Lord has shown Nineveh similar grace. Jonah's complaint reveals that his obedience to God's call has not been wholehearted. Jonah continues to think that God has acted in bad faith in forgiving the Ninevites.

The dialogue that follows Jonah's complaint between the prophet and the Lord allows the narrator to explore more fully the main themes of the text. First, the reader gets a glimpse into God's motives for showing compassion to the Ninevites. Second, the narrator contrasts the human desire for retribution with God's propensity for mercy. Just as God provided a fish to rescue Jonah from drowning, God now provides a plant, a worm, and a hot wind as further object lessons meant to help rescue Jonah from his own lack of mercy. The cliffhanger of an ending prevents the reader from knowing how Jonah ultimately responded but invites readers to consider their own responses to God's mercy toward the worst of sinners. God's dialogue with Jonah also goads a reluctant audience to consider their attitudes toward evildoers. Do they wish for anything other than retribution in the lives of their oppressors? If not, what does it mean for God's people to refuse to follow God's ways in their dealings with evildoers?

JONAH'S COMPLAINT, 4:1-3

Jonah, who has been missing in action since the beginning of chapter 3, suddenly reappears with a scowl. God's merciful actions toward Nineveh greatly displease the prophet. In his displeasure, Jonah burns with anger (4:1). His reaction contradicts God's actions at the end of chapter 3. When God saw that Nineveh turned from their *evil* ways, God relented from bringing *evil* upon them. God's mercy now appears to Jonah as *evil*. The Hebrew word translated *evil* or *calamity* in 3:10 is the same Hebrew word used to convey extreme displeasure in 4:1. God relented from bringing disaster on the Ninevites. Jonah saw this lack of disaster as the true disaster. He wanted the Ninevites punished. Furthermore, the Ninevites prayed in hope God would relent from his "fierce anger" (3:9). God relented, but now Jonah is fiercely angry over God's lack of anger (4:1). The Hebrew word for *anger* in these verses conveys the idea of one who glows hot.[1] Jonah's anger burns brightly throughout this chapter (4:1, 4, 9). In fact, anger proves to be Jonah's defining characteristic at the close of this story.

In 4:2, Jonah prays for the second time in this short book. In his first prayer, Jonah offered a psalm of Thanksgiving in response to his deliverance from death. In that psalm, Jonah's praise culminated with the declaration, "Deliverance belongs to the LORD!" (2:9). Ironically, Jonah now voices a full-throated complaint concerning God's deliverance of the Ninevites. Jonah's confession clears up some of the mysteries in the text. The reader is finally informed about Jonah's motives for fleeing God's presence in 1:3. Jonah knew back then that God would likely forgive the Ninevites. Jonah simply could not stomach the idea. In his mind, the Ninevites were too wicked to be forgiven.

In Jonah's complaint, the reader learns he voiced his objection to God back in Israel. How did Jonah know ahead of time that God would forgive the Ninevites? Some have suggested that because Jonah was a prophet, he could see the future. The narrator provides no indication God granted Jonah a vision of what would happen after he preached against the Ninevites. Jonah's confession in 4:2, however, makes it clear Jonah did not need to see the future to know what would occur. He could predict God's future actions because he knew God's character. Jonah describes God as gracious, merciful, slow to anger, abounding in steadfast love, and ready to relent in punishing (4:2). His words echo God's self-description in Exodus 34:6-7. These words serve as a confession

Describing God

Jonah's description of God in 4:2 can be found in one form or another throughout the Hebrew Scriptures. James Limburg provides a helpful chart that compares and contrasts Jonah's use of this description with other places in the Bible.

Scripture Text	Compassionate/ gracious	Merciful	Slow to anger	Abounding in love	Changing mind
Jonah 4:2	X	X	X	X	X
Joel 2:13	X	X	X	X	X
Psalm 145:8	X	X	X	X	–
Nehemiah 9:17	X	X	X	X	–
Exodus 34:6-7	X	X	X	X	–
Psalms 86:15	X	X	X	X	–
Psalm 103:8	X	X	X	X	–
Psalm 111:4	X	X	–	–	–
2 Chronicles 30:9	X	X	–	–	–
Numbers 14:18	–	–	X	X	–
Nehemiah 9:31	X	X	–	–	–

Source: James Limburg, *Jonah*, Old Testament Library (Louisville KY: Westminster/John Knox, 1993) 90.

of faith for ancient Hebrews, showing up repeatedly in the Hebrew Scriptures. Jonah believes these words accurately describe his God. He has been grateful for these characteristics at work in his life, but he is appalled that God would act the same way toward the Ninevites.

Jonah's description of God is evocative. It not only draws from the Hebrews' rich history with God but also accurately describes the God the reader meets in this book. First, God is both gracious and merciful. These two words mean almost the same thing. Both words can be translated as *compassion*. The first, *ḥannun*, appears thirteen times in the Hebrew Scriptures and is used only of God. The second, *raḥam*, carries the idea of a mother's care and concern for the child in her womb.[2] The combined image speaks of a God who looks upon Israel with loving, compassionate, merciful favor. God's willingness to rescue Jonah despite Jonah's petulance gives evidence that God is a merciful parent. The image of God as a compassionate parent makes sense when one speaks of God's actions toward Israel, but the image would have alarmed the original audience when applied to God's relationship with the wicked Ninevites.

Next, God is slow to anger. The Hebrew idiom is literally "long of nostrils" and indicates that a person is "open, warm, and generous."[3] The phrase most often describes God's nature, but the book of Proverbs also lifts up this kind of patience as a virtue of the wise (Prov 14:29; 15:18; 16:32). God has clearly been slow to anger with Jonah. Jonah has actively attempted to thwart God's plans. Still, God has remained patient with him. Jonah does not return the favor; he burns with anger toward God and wishes God would cease to be patient with Nineveh.

The most evocative word for the early reader had to be the description of God "abounding in steadfast love." The Hebrew word for this is *ḥesed*. If *agape* proves to be the best description of God's self-giving love in the New Testament, *ḥesed* covers similar ground in the Hebrew Scriptures. Notoriously difficult to translate into English, the word *ḥesed* conveys the idea of God's unyielding covenantal loyalty to Israel. It can be translated as *loving-kindness, faithfulness, loyalty,* and even *grace.* It is the kind of love that God shows Israel time and time again. In some ways, it could be described simply as God's love for Israel.

Biblical Figures Call on God to Take Their Lives

Other biblical characters who ask God to kill them face far more drastic circumstances than did Jonah. Job, for example, demands that God take his life in response to the loss he has experienced and his inability to get an adequate response from God (6:9-14). In Jer 20:14-18, the prophet laments his life because of the shame he is forced to bear. Samson asks God for strength so that he might die in one final act of vengeance after the Philistines had brutalized him (Judg 16:28-31). By comparison, Jonah's call for God to take his life appears trivial, a petulant and childish response to his momentary discomfort.

Remarkably, Jonah expected God to show this kind of love to the Ninevites even as he recoiled at the thought.

Finally, God is ready to relent from punishing. God's posture toward Israel has always included a readiness to forgive. God is slow to anger. Even when provoked, God's anger does not last forever, for God "delights in showing clemency" (Mic 7:18). Again, Jonah has experienced God's forgiveness firsthand. Before the Ninevites received their second chance, Jonah received his. Jonah knows that God is gracious because God has proven so in both Israel's history and Jonah's life. Jonah simply cannot stomach the fact that God would act in the same way toward Nineveh.

The author does not explain exactly why God's actions bother Jonah, only that they do. The extent of his frustration is made clear in 4:3 when he asks God to end his life. In 1:12, Jonah sought death over obedience. He had not wanted to participate in the Ninevites' deliverance. Now that he has reluctantly aided in their salvation, he asks God to put him out of his misery. The Hebrew

Scriptures contain a number of people who ask God to take their lives. Moses grows so burdened by the task of leading a grumbling people through the desert that he says to God, "Put me to death at once—if I have found favor in your sight" (Num 11:15). Elijah also asks God to end his life after fleeing the threats of Jezebel (1 Kgs 19:14). Moses and Elijah sound like leaders who are emotionally and physically drained. Jonah sounds like a spoiled brat. He would rather die than be associated with a God who forgives Ninevites.

Jonah's embarrassment at God's mercy anticipates the reaction of the older brother in Jesus' story of the prodigal son (Luke 15:11-32). Like Jonah, the older brother became angry when he witnessed the mercy the father had extended to the sinful younger brother. The older brother did not ask to die, but he did refuse to go into the party the father threw to celebrate the younger brother's homecoming. The older brother did not want to be caught dead at such a ridiculous display of generosity. Jonah prefers death to being a participant in an equally audacious display of mercy.

Some ancient manuscripts indicate a pause in the text after Jonah's request to die.[4] Regardless of the motive, it should cause us to pause any time a prophet of the Lord wishes to die. God rescued Jonah when he cried out to the Lord as his life ebbed away. How will the Lord respond when Jonah cries out to die?

GOD QUESTIONS JONAH'S RIGHT TO BE ANGRY, 4:4-9

God initially responds by asking Jonah a question: "Is it right for you to be angry?" Jonah's anger surfaces in 4:1, and the same word is repeated here in verse 4. In both instances, the word conveys the idea of burning up with anger. The obvious answer to the Lord's question is "no." The Lord may do as the Lord pleases. Jonah, as a servant of the Lord, is in no position to judge the Lord's actions, much less be angered by them. God's question echoes the question the Lord asked Cain in Genesis 4:6 after Cain grew angry at God's rejection of Cain's offering. As humans, we may believe we have good reasons for our anger. As humans, we have little right to be angry with God for doing as God pleases. As Cain's story illustrates, those who persist in anger toward God often find sin lurking at their doors.

Explaining Jonah's Response in 4:5

J. M. Sasson provides a thorough assessment of the history of interpretation of this verse, along with helpful categories for explaining the problem of the location of the verse: textual corruption, grammatical readjustment, and explanations of the text "as is." Those who see 4:5 as a textual problem generally suggest either omitting the verse (K. Budde, J. Bewer) or relocating it to its "original" position following 3:4 (H. Winckler, E. Bickerman, and P. Trible—although this proposal was first suggested in the Middle Ages). Those who argue for grammatical readjustment (e.g., H. Wolff, P. Weimar) translate the verse as a pluperfect and treat it as a parenthetical flashback. They claim that the scene forces the reader to read the scene as happening simultaneously with the Ninevite reaction to Jonah's preaching. Sasson correctly notes this is highly unusual because of the Hebrew construction. Some treat the text "as is" (e.g., J. Magonet and J. Sasson). Magonet explains the tension

from the structural parallel of Jonah's flight to Tarshish in chapter 1. Sasson suggests a purely literary role—to put Jonah east of the city to make him the first one to feel the heat from the east wind.

Jack M. Sasson, *Jonah* (AB 24B; New York: Doubleday, 1990) 287–89; 139.

Karl Budde, "The Book of Jonah," in *Jewish Encyclopedia* (New York: Funk and Wagnall, 1904) 7:227–30.

Julius Bewer, *Jonah* (ICC; Edinburgh: T & T Clark) 58–59.

Hugo Winckler, "Zum Buche Jona," *Altorientalische Forschungen* 2:260–65.

Elias J. Bickerman, "Les Deux Erreurs du prophèt Jonas," *Revue d'histoire et de philosophie religieuses* 45 (1965): 232–64.

Phyllis Trible, "Studies in the Book of Jonah," (Ph.D. diss., Columbia University; Ann Arbor, University Microfilm International, 1963.

Hans Walter Wolff, *Obadiah and Jonah* (trans. Margaret Kohl; Continental Commentary; Minneapolis: Augsburg, 1976) 163, 169.

Peter Weimar, "Jon 4,5. Beobachtungen zur Entstehung der Jonaerzählung," *Biblische Notizen* 18 (1982): 86–109.

Jonathan Magonet, *Form and Meaning: Studies in Literary Techniques in the Book of Jonah* (Beiträge zur biblischen Exegese und Theologie 2; Bern: Herbert Lang, 1976) 5–860.

What is obvious to the reader may or may not be obvious to Jonah. We do not know because Jonah does not respond verbally to the Lord's answer. Instead, he answers God's question by moving to another location. Jonah's move out of the city is not as drastic as his flight from the Lord's presence in 1:3. His move does, however, have the effect of avoiding a conversation with God.

The text reports that upon leaving the city, Jonah made a booth for shade and then sat down in order to "see what would become of the city" (4:5). Jonah's actions are a bit puzzling. Jonah already knows that God has forgiven the city and is angry about that fact (4:1). Some scholars hypothesize that the remainder of the book flashes back to a previous conversation between Jonah and the Lord. Nothing in the text, though, suggests it is intended to be read back into the story. As the story is presented, Jonah simply appears to be sulking and perhaps holding out hope that God will change God's mind once more and punish the city.

Throughout the Hebrew Scriptures, booths serve as temporary shelters. Jacob built them for his cattle (Gen 33:17); soldiers spent time in them on the field of battle (1 Kgs 20:12, 16). Guards took residence in them outside vineyards (Job 27:18; Isa 1:8). Most frequently, the Hebrew Scriptures mention booths in the context of the Festival of Booths (Lev 23:33-43). During this festival, Jews built temporary shelters of tree branches as a reminder of the way people lived during the wilderness wanderings. Jonah's hut does not appear to have any connection to the festival, but it does indicate he intended to stay and watch the city for an extended period. God has questioned Jonah's right to be angry. Jonah's response is to pitch a tent and stew.

If Jonah's actions are an attempt to teach God a lesson, God returns the favor. Just as God appointed the fish to swallow Jonah, God now appoints a bush to grow up over the prophet (4:6). The word translated "bush" appears only this one time in the Scriptures, making the exact species impossible to determine. Traditionally, interpreters, noting the speed with which these plants grow and the shade they can produce, have suggested that the bush was either a climbing gourd or a castor bean. Attempts to identify the species of plant miss the point. Just as readers need not worry about what kind of fish can swallow a man whole, neither do they need to be concerned about what kind of plant can grow so quickly. Both the fish and the plant point toward God's involvement in the story, not scientific reasonability.

The *qîqāyôn* **Plant**

(Credit: Joaquim Alves Gaspar, http://en.wikipedia.org/wiki/File:Ricinus_March_2010-1.jpg)

Linguistically, Jonah's author may not have intended a castor bean plant (pictured here). The LXX, Syriac, and Vulgate point to other interpretations. The LXX (*kolokuntha*) and Syriac versions interpret the plant as a gourd, while the Vulgate translates it as ivy (*hedera*). The common denominator of all these suggestions is the leafy foliage.

God appoints the plant to grow and provide shade over the prophet to teach the prophet a lesson. Jonah's self-built booth fails to shelter him adequately. God's miraculous provision of the plant "saves" Jonah from his discomfort. Once again, God saves Jonah even though Jonah does not deserve to be saved. Jonah, who had been burning with anger since 4:1, now becomes "very happy about the bush." English translations downplay the dramatic reversal. Jonah was "displeased with great displeasure." Now Jonah "rejoiced with great joy."[5] Sasson points out that Jonah may have perceived the plant as a concession from God that Jonah's complaints were valid. If this is the case, Jonah's happiness about the bush may indicate more than gratitude for the shade. Jonah's joy may indicate that he viewed the plant as a sign of "a renewed understanding between the two."[6] Prioritizing personal comfort over concern for others, he may have simply been grateful for the shade.

Worm

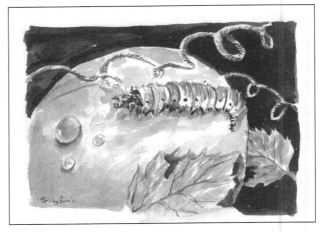

(Credit: Barclay Burns)

This worm appears in several other OT contexts. It is the same pest that feasts on grapes in Deut 28:39, appears in the rotting manna in Exod 16:20, and consumes human flesh in Isa 14:11; 66:24. The worm, generally thought to be the common fruit grub pictured here (known as *Eupoecilia ambiguella, clysia ambiguella,* or *cochylis ambiguella*), grows only to a length of around 18 mm (*less than 3/4 inch*). The worm is red and served as a base ingredient in old red dyes, thus explaining the use of the same term for "red material" in several texts in the Priestly material of Exodus referring to red elements in the tabernacle (Exod 25:4; 26:1, 31, 36; 27:16; 28:5, 6, 8, 15, 33; 35:6, 23, 25, 35; 36:8, 35, 37; 38:18, 23; 39:1, 2, 3; 39:5. 8, 24, 29).

In 4:7, a new day has begun, and Jonah remains under the plant. Jonah may think that God's positive response in sending the plant is an indication that God will yet move in Jonah's direction and punish the Ninevites. God does no such thing. Instead, God now appoints a worm to attack the bush so that it withers. Like the fish and the plant, the worm has acted at the Lord's bidding. God has not finished with this object lesson. As the sun rises, the Lord appoints a hot east wind to disturb Jonah's comfort. Hot winds in that part of the world (called the *scirocco*) are said to cause "exhaustion, depression, feelings of unreality, and occasionally, bizarre behavior."[7] These winds likely blow away any remains of Jonah's shelter, so he is now exposed to the elements. Just as the worm attacked the plant, now the sun attacks Jonah's head. With the sun beating down on his head and a hot wind blowing in his face, Jonah experiences something akin to sunstroke.

Once more, Jonah asks to die, saying, "It is better for me to die than to live." There are clear echoes of the Elijah story mentioned above. The phrase "he asked that he might die" is the same in both passages (Jonah 4:8; 1 Kgs 19:4). Furthermore, in both instances, an exhausted prophet experienced a prolonged depression. After a rest, Elijah does not ask to die a second time, but he does continue to complain to the Lord (1 Kgs 19:10). After a full night's sleep, Jonah does more than complain; he repeats his previous declaration that it is better for him to die than to live (4:3; 4:8). God's intervention has not moved the prophet one bit.

In 4:9, God asks again about Jonah's right to be angry: "Is it right for you to be angry about the bush?" The repetition of the question suggests it is fundamental to understanding this chapter if not the whole book. The first time God asked Jonah this question, Jonah refused to answer. Even Jonah knew it would be imprudent to acknowledge out loud that he was angry over the sparing of Nineveh. This time God's question is not about Nineveh but about the plant. Jonah either does not recognize the trap or is simply tired of playing the game. He answers forcefully that he has every right to be angry, even angry enough to die.

If Jonah's concern is only for personal comfort, then his reaction is beyond the pale. If, as Sasson argues, Jonah saw the plant as a sign of God's approval, then his anger might be a result of feeling he is once more on the outs with the Almighty. What is worse, the still un-scorched Ninevites remain in God's favor. God's actions toward the Ninevites combined with God's removal of the plant may feel like the ultimate betrayal to Jonah. God's provision in the past don't matter to Jonah; he, the prophet of the Lord, suffers while the wicked Ninevites enjoy the Lord's kindness.

In either case, Jonah proves to be woefully shortsighted. As God will point out, Jonah has much to learn about mercy. Jonah also has much to learn about God. God has provided or appointed a fish, a plant, a worm, and wind in Jonah's life. Might God appoint yet another thing to bring Jonah relief? The fish came as Jonah cried out to God for mercy. Would God act again if Jonah called out once more for help? We do not know because Jonah does not ask for help. He asks to die.

GOD'S FINAL WORD, 4:9-10

God responds to Jonah's protest with a short sermon. In this sermon, God uses a minor point in order to argue a more significant one. Rabbinic teachers frequently used this method of arguing, known as *qal wāḥōmer*.[8] It is the method Jesus used when he argued, "If you then, who are evil, know how to give good gifts to your children, how much more will your Father in heaven give good things to those who ask him!" (Matt 7:11). The argument works by getting someone to concede the minor point, which then logically leads to the more significant assertion.

Compassion

AΩ The Hebrew word *ḥesed* means "to show compassion upon." The NRSV translates the verb here (and in 4:11) as "concerned about," presumably to avoid the idea that one would show emotion toward a plant (see also Sasson, 309). However, the caricature of Jonah's compassion seems to be precisely the point of the text, given that God uses the same verb in 4:11 to imply his "concern" for the living beings of Nineveh.

Jack M. Sasson, *Jonah* (AB 24B; New York: Doubleday, 1990).

God's minor point is simple; Jonah is concerned about the plant. He did not contribute to this plant's growth, but still the plant's destruction has caused Jonah great concern primarily because its loss has brought him physical discomfort. Jonah, who believes in his right to feel concern for the plant, has already conceded this point, so God moves on to the major premise. If Jonah feels concern for a small thing like a plant, is it not within God's rights to feel concern for Nineveh? Nineveh, after all, is not a small thing but a great city—a point emphasized throughout the text (1:2; 3:2, 3). The destruction of the city, more specifically the human beings within it, would be a loss for God.

God highlights Nineveh's population. Beyond the more than 120,000 people, there are also many animals that also fasted and wore sackcloth (3:8).

Population of Nineveh

Jonah 4:11 indicates that Nineveh had more than 120,000 persons. This number is not impossibly large for later times, but is likely too large for the time in which the prophet Jonah actually lived. By some estimates, ancient Nineveh could have had a population of well over 300,000 at the height of its power in the seventh century. To put this number in perspective, Jerusalem *increased* in size to 24,000 when refugees from Samaria fled to it in the latter eighth century.

James D. Nogalski, *The Book of the Twelve: Hosea–Jonah*, Smyth & Helwys Bible Commentary (Macon GA: Smyth & Helwys, 2011) 450.

Are not the animals more important than Jonah's plant? God's point is clear: living beings matter to God. Concern for others has been a theme of the book. The captain of the ship showed concern for his crew (1:6). The king of Nineveh showed concern for the people of his city (3:8). Neither wanted those in their care to perish. These pagan leaders anticipate God's concern. God is concerned for the Ninevites.

As difficult as it might be for Jonah to understand, even the Ninevites are in God's care. The Ninevites desperately need someone to care for them. God explains that they do not know their right from their left. The phrase can indicate innocence though that is not likely the meaning here. God has already spoken of their wickedness (1:2). More likely, the phrase implies that the people are helpless or even pitiful. They are sheep without a shepherd. Their wicked, violent lives fall far short of God's intentions for humanity. Limburg notes that the verb translated "to be concerned" or "to care" in 4:11 "means literally having tears in one's eyes."[9] The trouble the Ninevites have brought on themselves does not cause God to rejoice. God grieves instead. God looks over Nineveh in much the same way that Jesus would look over Jerusalem and weep (Luke 19:41-44).

In Hebrew, the length of God's speech (4:10-11) matches Jonah's at the beginning of the chapter (4:2-3).[10] Both speeches help the reader understand this book. Jonah's speech, though a complaint, clearly confesses that YHWH is a God of compassion, mercy, and love. God's speech explains why God acts in those ways even toward the Ninevites. God's explanation ends in the form

---

Rhetorical Question

In actuality, 4:11 does not contain explicit interrogative markers. It is, however, universally recognized as a rhetorical question because of its close syntactical connection to the previous verse and the manner in which its content would otherwise contradict the point of 4:10. This construction is common in biblical Hebrew.

See Wilhelm Gesenius, Emil E. Kautzsch, and Arthur Ernest Cowley, *Gesenius' Hebrew Grammar* (repr. 1970; Oxford; Clarendon, 1910), §150a.

God's Compassion on Creation

Rüdiger Lux points out that the question with which Jonah ends makes a profound statement about the nature of YHWH's compassion and justice. He says,

God does not base compassion on a human act of piety (confession) or goodness (repentance); nor on religion or morality. God's grace and compassion are the grace of creation (*Schöpfungsgnade*), born from God's uncoerced devotion to God's creatures.

Rüdiger Lux, *Jona: Prophet zwischen 'Verweigerung' und 'Gehorsam'* (Forschungen zur Religion und Literatur des Alten und Neuen Testaments; Göttingen: Vandenhoeck und Ruprecht, 1994) 162 (my translation).

of a rhetorical question. The question is as much for the reader as it is for Jonah. The open-ended nature of the conclusion of this book leaves the reader asking, "Whose vision of the world will I embrace, Jonah's or God's?" Jonah's last words insist upon one's rights even unto death. They are words of spite, anger, and hate. God's last words graciously convey deep concern for creatures both great and small.

TEACHING THIS CHAPTER

The fourth chapter of Jonah contains the heart of the book's message: God's primary posture toward human beings is one of love and compassion. Jonah's description of God in 4:2, which draws on God's self-disclosure in Exodus 34:5-6, is accurate at all times and for all people, including people as wicked as the Ninevites. If God were not compassionate toward Nineveh, then God's self-description in Exodus 34:5-6 would not simply be incomplete; it would be false. God's compassion toward the Ninevites reveals God's self-description to be true. God cares for even the worst among us. So too, then, should we. Helping a class grasp the difficulty of this message depends on the teacher's ability to explain why Jonah was angry about Nineveh's reprieve. It's also helpful to provide opportunities to for the class to talk through what it might mean for us to love others as God loves us.

Why Was Jonah Angry with God?

In chapter 4, readers finally learn why Jonah originally fled God's presence. He foresaw that God was going to forgive the Ninevites, and he did not want to contribute to their salvation. When God finally does forgive the Ninevites as a result of Jonah's preaching, Jonah burns with anger. The reader knows that Jonah is angry that the Ninevites escape judgment, but the exact reasons for his anger are not spelled out. Some argue Jonah is upset that God's change of plans casts Jonah as a false prophet. Jonah preached that Nineveh would burn and then it did not. This might be the case, but it seems a minor point. Furthermore, Jonah's actual sermon was ambiguous. Jonah's words in 3:4 could mean either that Nineveh would be overthrown or that they would be transformed. Nineveh was transformed not through fire and brimstone but through repentance. In this sense, Jonah's sermon came true even if it did not come true in the manner Jonah originally intended it.

Jonah's anger derives from the fact that Nineveh was spared, but why did Jonah want them destroyed? In previous centuries, commentators have emphasized the fact that the Ninevites were non-Jews. These commentators use Jonah as an example of Jewish exclusivism. This dangerous line of interpretation does not take into account all the information we have. Jonah did not hate all Gentiles. His behavior toward the sailors shows that he did not hate all non-Jews. Jonah even volunteered to sacrifice his life for the sake of the Gentile sailors (1:12). When commentators ignore Jonah's nuanced response to non-Jews, they run the risk of contributing to anti-Semitism by stereotyping Jews as anti-Gentile.

The most likely explanation for Jonah's anger involves his acute sense of justice. For Jonah, and many others who suffered at the hands of the Assyrians, the crimes of the Ninevites could not be forgiven if the world hoped to retain any sense of justice. The book of Jonah highlights not the Ninevites' idolatry but rather their violence and wickedness. History records the atrocities of the Assyrians. Jonah and his readers would have viewed the Assyrians as oppressors. God, Jonah likely protested, was supposed to be on the side of the oppressed rather than the oppressor. Fretheim is likely right when he argues, "The basic issue between God and Jonah then is the question of God's justice."[11] For Jonah, God grants mercy so liberally that any sensible concept of justice comes undone.

Ancient Assyria no longer causes modern readers to recoil in horror. We have our own people who qualify as the worst of the worst. Take for instance the Nazis, who exterminated six million Jews during World War II. In 1943, Simon Wiesenthal was taken from Lemberg Concentration Camp, where he was a prisoner, and moved into town to work in the army hospital. While he was working at the hospital, a mortally wounded SS soldier called the young Jewish man to his side. The soldier began confessing the horrific crimes he had committed against Jews, including the burning to death of more than 150 Jews locked inside a house. At the end of his story, the SS soldier turned to Wiesenthal and begged forgiveness. Without saying a word, Wiesenthal stood up and walked out.

Wiesenthal retells this story in much greater detail in the first half of his book *The Sunflower*.[12] In the second half of the book, he turns his attention to the reader, asking, "Was my silence at the bedside of the dying Nazi right or wrong?" Wiesenthal asks the question open-mindedly. He tells of genuinely having struggled with his choice for many years. In pursuit of an answer, the book enlists other people's responses. Fifty-three theologians, politicians, writers, Holocaust survivors, and survivors of other more recent genocides provided essays. As expected, there is no real consensus as to whether or not Wiesenthal's refusal to forgive was morally right or wrong.

The Sunflower is a challenging read, not just because of the atrocities it reports but also because of the questions it poses. Who is qualified to offer forgiveness? What does it mean to forgive? Are some evils unforgivable? Obviously, these are not easy questions to answer. Even if we decide that people should be forgiven, those answers are more difficult to live out. Wiesenthal's struggle perhaps makes us a little more sympathetic to Jonah's anger and a little more honest about our own struggles to forgive. For instance, what does it mean in our day to forgive those whose evil etched September 11, 2001, forever in our consciousness?

Compassion: God's Response to the Human Predicament

Just as the book of Jonah leaves the prophet's questions concerning God's justice primarily in the background, so too does it leave aside any lengthy attempts to justify God's actions. Instead, the book simply argues that compassion is an essential component of God's character. When God gets angry, God's anger is a byproduct of divine compassion. God does not want anyone to face destruction. What we experience as divine anger is often God resisting our self-destructive behaviors. God is ready to show compassion to all people, including the most wicked among us.

If we have a problem with God forgiving those we hate, our anger serves as a sign that we have forgotten our place as creatures. God is free to show grace to whomever God pleases. We are in no place to argue with God about God's actions toward others. We remember our place when we recall that everything we have is by God's grace. Jonah was alive by God's grace. Jonah was a part of Israel by God's grace. Israel was God's people not through any merit of its own, but by God's grace. The deep concern God has shown us is the same concern God has for all people.

The story of Jonah hopes to do more than compel us to grudgingly accept that God can forgive whomever God pleases. The story of Jonah and the Lord

---

The End Is Reconciliation

We have before us the glorious opportunity to inject a new dimension of love into the veins of our civilization. There is still a voice crying out in terms that echo across the generations, saying: "Love your enemies, bless them that curse you, pray for them that despitefully use you, that you may be the children of your Father which is in Heaven." This love might well be the salvation of our civilization. This is why I am so impressed with our motto for the week, "Freedom and Justice through Love." Not through violence; not through hate; no not even through boycotts; but through love. It is true that as we struggle for freedom in America we will have to boycott at times. But we must remember as we boycott that a boycott is not an end within itself; it is merely a means to awaken a sense of shame within the oppressor and challenge his false sense of superiority. But the end is reconciliation; the end is redemption; the end is the creation of the beloved community. It is this type of spirit and this type of love that can transform opponents into friends. It is this type of understanding goodwill that will transform the deep gloom of the old age into the exuberant gladness of the new age. It is this love which will bring about miracles in the hearts of men.

Dr. Martin Luther King, Jr., "Facing the Challenge of a New Age," an address to the Montgomery Improvement Association's Institute on Nonviolence and Social Change at Hold Street Baptist Church on December 3, 1956, http://mlk-kpp01.stanford.edu/kingweb/publications/papers/vol3/561203.000-Facing_the_Challenge_of_a_New_Age,_annual_address_at_the_first_annual_Institute_on_Nonviolence_and_Social_Change.htm.

---

attempts to move us toward the practice of God's compassion in the world today. It does this first and foremost by humanizing the oppressor. One of the tools of oppression is the dehumanizing of victims. You cannot slaughter millions of people without first dehumanizing them. Examples abound today of entire categories of people who have been dehumanized by dominant cultures. What we often fail to understand is that those who practice oppression also suffer from the dehumanizing effects of sin.

In their sin, oppressors become less than human, or at least less than God intended humans to be. It is easy for those who have been oppressed to see their oppressors as monsters, as less than human.[13] In the perversity of sin, victims commit the same error as their oppressors when they see their oppressors as beings less than human. Because victims no longer see their oppressors as human, they justify any form of revenge. When the tables are turned, victims frequently trade places with their oppressors and the cycle of oppression continues unabated.

What can be done? First, we must recognize that God views both victim and oppressor through the lens of compassion and love. God stands against all evil, but not against evildoers. In fact, God stands against evil because God is for the people who do evil. God wants to redeem human beings from being both the victims and the perpetrators of evil. The book of Jonah affirms that God experiences all human beings' descent into sin as a loss. Jonah felt concern or worry over the loss of the plant. God feels concern or worry over the loss of *any* human being, including those who are as wicked as the Ninevites. God grieves both the harm a terrorist does to others and the harm the terrorist does to his own soul. God's aim, then, is not the defeat or destruction of evildoers. Instead, God longs to defeat evil via the redemption of evildoers. In other words, God wants to overthrow Nineveh, but not in the way that Jonah hopes. Jonah wants justice. God desires reconciliation.

Reconciliation to God and one another requires two actions: repentance and forgiveness. Both actions play a major role in the story of Jonah. Attempts at reconciliation that do not account for sin do not bring about reconciliation; instead, they perpetuate injustice. For true reconciliation to occur, evil must be named for what it is. Only then can forgiveness be offered.

How can we forgive our oppressors? In his excellent book *Exclusion and Embrace*, Miroslav Volf argues that the path to offering forgiveness begins with the recognition that we, too, stand in need of forgiveness. Volf, a Croatian theologian who witnessed firsthand the atrocities of the Serbian war, notes that Jesus brought a radical message to an oppressed people: "Repent!" It makes sense to us that Jesus would deliver this message to the oppressors of God's people, but why did Jesus deliver a message of repentance to the victims of oppression? Volf argues that Jesus was not blaming the victims. Rather, he was calling them to lay aside the values of the oppressor altogether:

> To repent means to resist the seductiveness of the sinful values and practices and to let the new order of God's reign be established in one's heart. For a victim to repent means not to allow the oppressors to determine the terms under which the social conflict is carried out . . . . Repentance thus empowers victims and disempowers the oppressors. It "humanizes" the victims precisely by protecting them from either mimicking or dehumanizing the oppressors. Far from being a sign of acquiescence to the dominant order, repentance creates a haven of God's new world in the midst of the old and so makes the transformation of the old possible.[14]

Jonah's inability to repent leads to his enslavement. Jonah becomes what he hates. For in his dehumanizing hatred of the Ninevites, he participates in the very evil that he condemns. The Ninevites have dehumanized others. Now, Jonah dehumanizes them. Repentance of his own sin would not excuse the Ninevites' sins. Rather, repentance would help prevent Jonah from being co-opted by the dehumanizing effect of oppression.

The idea that God embraces those who oppress us is offensive. There is no way around this. From a human perspective, Jonah has every right to be offended that God would forgive the Ninevites of their sin. From our human perspective, we fail to understand how God can be both for us and for those who harm us. From God's perspective, *all* human beings stand in need of God's forgiving grace. This is the offense of the cross. Christ died not simply for the sins of one group of people. Christ died for all. Sin is universal, yet God has a universal love for all people. If we want no part of God's embrace of our enemies, then, like Jonah, we will be left resisting the embrace of God.

QUESTIONS FOR REFLECTION AND DISCUSSION

1. When God forgave the Ninevites, Jonah burned with anger. Do you think Jonah had a right to be angry? Why or why not?
2. Can you think of a time when an offer of forgiveness made you angry? Why do you think you felt this way?
3. I once heard a Cuban immigrant say on a television report that if Fidel Castro made it to heaven, she would rather go to hell. How is that attitude similar to Jonah's? Is there anyone or any group of people that makes you feel the same way? If so, why?
4. Why is the practice of recognizing our enemy's humanity important? In what ways can we resist the urge to dehumanize our enemies? Conversely, in what ways can we recognize the humanity of our enemies?
5. The book of Jonah stresses God's compassion for the worst of sinners as represented by the Ninevites. Who qualifies as the worst of sinners in our world? How can the church practice compassion toward them?

SUGGESTIONS FOR WORSHIP AND PREACHING

Order of Worship

Call to Worship
Come let us worship the Lord, our God.
Merciful and gracious,
Slow to anger,

Quick to forgive.
Abounding in love,
Faithful forever.

"Praise, My Soul, the King of Heaven" (Graham Kendrick & Martin Smith, Thankyou Music, 2013, adapted from words by H. F. Lyte [1793–1847])

"Grace Greater than Our Sin"

New Testament Reading: Matthew 5:43-48

"Have Thine Own Way, Lord" (Verses 1, 2, and 4)

Moment of Prayer for Our Enemies

"Have Thine Own Way, Lord (Verse 1, reprise)

Choral Hymn: "Compassion Hymn" (Keith Getty, Kristyn Getty, and Stuart Townend/arr. Craig Courtney, Alfred Music, 2010)

Sermon: It's a Question of Right and Wrong

"Rescue the Perishing"

Benediction: May you have the power, with all the Lord's holy people, to grasp how wide and long and high and deep is the love of Christ, and to know this love that surpasses knowledge—that you may be filled to the measure of all the fullness of God. Amen.

Example Sermon Outline: It's a Question of Right and Wrong

Introduction

Leif Enger's novel *Peace Like a River* recounts the story of Jeremiah Land, a custodian for the small, rural school his children attend. Principal Holgren, Jeremiah's boss, does everything in his power to make Jeremiah's life miserable. Mr. Holgren's face, "a minefield of red boils," matches his personality. One day, Mr. Holgren's meanness toward Jeremiah spills over, and he fires the custodian in front of the whole school and falsely accuses him of drunkenness. One of Jeremiah's sons, Reuben, sees it all. He feels an immense hatred toward Mr. Holgren welling up in his bones. Jeremiah, for his part, walks over to the man who has just fired him. Instead of lashing out in anger, Jeremiah gently touches the man's face and then walks away. Reuben cannot believe what he sees. He is not shocked the man's face is healed; he knows of his father's special gift. He simply cannot stomach that his dad has chosen to extend that gift to the man who fired him. Reuben explains, "Listen: There are easier things than witnessing a miracle of God. For his part, Mr. Holgren didn't know what to make of it; he looked horrified; the new peace in his hide didn't sink deep; he covered his face from view and slunk from the cafeteria. I knew what had happened, though. I knew exactly what to make of it, and it made me mad enough to spit."[15]

Rueben is most certainly correct. There are easier things than witnessing a miracle of God, especially when those miracles benefit your enemy. Just ask Jonah. In our text today we find the prophet fuming mad because God has, miracle of miracles, forgiven the wicked Ninevites. Because most of us do not know any Ninevites, it is easy for us to judge Jonah. What kind of person gets angry at God's compassion? A normal one, if you ask me, especially if God's compassion involves letting the worst among us off scot-free! The Assyrians are some of history's worst bad guys. They delighted in doing evil. The prophet Nahum describes ancient Nineveh as a city full of lies and dead bodies. The Assyrians belong in the same camp as Nazis, drug kingpins, and ISIS soldiers. And God forgives them. All they have to do is repent, and God lets them off the hook.

Struggling with Grace

Jonah can't take it. He tells God this is what he was worried about all along. This is why he ran. He knew that God would forgive the Ninevites in the end. Jonah's reasoning is telling. As a prophet of the Lord, he knows that God is gracious, merciful, and slow to anger. God abounds in steadfast love and is always ready to back out on a promise to punish. Jonah knows this is how God described the divine self in Exodus 34:6-7. Jonah knows this is who God has proven to be in Israel's life ever since.

While we might think that God's unconditional love is always a good thing, Jonah feels as if God is being unfair. God is treating oppressors with the same kindness and mercy God offers toward victims. Jonah is not sure he wants to live in a world where scoundrels like the Ninevites do not have to pay for their sins. He tried to die in chapter 1 by having the sailors toss him in the sea. God graciously rescued him then, but now Jonah regrets that he was saved. Jonah asks God to take his life. "Better that I would have died," Jonah reasons, "than have to watch the Ninevites get saved." Jonah wants a world that plays by clearer moral rules. Jonah wants the good guys always to win and the bad guys to get their comeuppance. Jonah is uncompromisingly sure that he knows the difference between the two.

God does not dispute who the bad guys are in this scenario. At least, God does not dispute that the Ninevites fit into the category. It was God who first said that Jonah was to go and preach against Nineveh because of its wickedness. God does not even spend time attempting to convince Jonah of his sinfulness; God would have had plenty of material to work with! God certainly could have shown Jonah that he had received as much grace as the Ninevites. But God chooses to go another route altogether, asking simply, "Is it right for you to be angry?"

God's question about Jonah's anger echoes the question the Lord asked Cain in Genesis 4:6 after Cain grew angry at God's rejection of Cain's offering. As humans, we may believe that we have good reasons for our anger at God and our fellow human beings. When we compare how God treats us to how God treats others, it can seem completely unfair. Still, we don't have the right to be angry with God for doing as God pleases. This is especially true when it comes to God's right to accept those whom God wishes to accept. Cain may be angry with God, but he takes his anger out on Abel. As Cain's story illustrates, those who persist in anger toward God often find sin lurking at their doors (Gen 4:7). What sin lurks at Jonah's door? Jonah finds himself looking at the Ninevites in much the same way that the Ninevites once looked at him. He sees them as less than human.

A Lesson in Loss

God's question does not lead to any reflection on the part of the prophet. "Is it right for me to be angry?!" Jonah cannot believe that God is bringing him into this discussion. In Jonah's eyes, the argument is not about what is right or wrong for *Jonah* to do but rather what is right and wrong for *God* to do. After all, if God does not do what is right by punishing evildoers, what hope is there for the rest of us? The world has lost its moral bearings. Jonah's frustration only grows . . . he refuses even to answer God. Instead, he stomps to the top of a hill, pitches a tent, and waits to see what will happen to Nineveh. It's as if the prophet is goading God finally to do what is right.

Jonah cannot see the Ninevites through God's perspective. He wants God to see them from *his* perspective—as enemies. God wants Jonah to see the Ninevites from the divine perspective. Just as God appointed the fish to rescue Jonah from the deep, God appoints a plant to save Jonah from his discomfort. It must have been very hot, for the text reports that Jonah rejoices with great joy after the plant provides him shade. It may be that Jonah saw the plant as a sign God had changed God's mind once again and was now seeing things Jonah's way. After all, it was a miraculous plant, and it was now shading Jonah from the heat.

If Jonah thought God had changed God's mind, Jonah was mistaken. As soon as Jonah is comforted, God appoints a worm to come and attack the bush. Then God appoints a hot, suffocating east wind to blow against the prophet. As the sun attacks Jonah's head, the prophet grows faint, and once again he declares, "It is better for me to live than to die." You almost don't blame him. Even to an outsider, it seems as if God is just picking on him at this point. Jonah apparently feels the same way. When God then asks Jonah, "Is it right for you to be angry at the bush?" Jonah cannot help replying, "Yes. I am angry enough to die."

Jonah has taken the bait. God points out that the loss Jonah feels over the plant is real. It may even be justified. Jonah has pity or concern over the plant. God concedes it is right for Jonah to have concern over a living creature, even one as temporary and insignificant as a plant. God then points out that, if it is right to have concern over a plant, how much more appropriate is it for God to have concern over Nineveh? Nineveh is a large city with lots of animals and more than 120,000 people.

What's more, God explains that the Ninevites are people who do not know "their right hand from their left." God's words do not justify the Ninevites' evil or excuse them. God is not saying that the evil they have done can simply be excused. God insists that the Ninevites repent of their wicked ways. God does see the Ninevites' evil as a sign that they are utterly lost. The Ninevites are like sheep without a shepherd: dumb and pitiful. Their stupidity has resulted in immense cruelty, and that cruelty has diminished their humanity in both their own eyes and in the eyes of their victims. However, God still sees in them the divine image. Losing them to evil, even evil of their own making, would cause God to experience the deepest of loss.

Conclusion: Whom Will We Follow?

God wants Jonah to understand that the Ninevites matter to God. I am not sure that Jonah understands. After God's sermon, the text falls silent. We do not know how Jonah responds. Perhaps Jonah's response is not the point of the story. Like all good stories, the story of Jonah and the Lord points us to the more contemporary story of "me and the Lord." Like Jonah, we each have people in our lives who qualify as Ninevites—people who have harmed us or who want to harm us; people who have belittled us and put us down; people who have failed to see the image of God in us and dehumanized us. The story of Jonah asks us difficult questions: How will we see our enemies? Will we dehumanize them in return? Will we see them as monsters who live beyond the reach of God's care? Or will we follow the way of our God, who loved even the Ninevites? Will we follow the one who, as he hung from the cross, declared, "Father, forgive them, for they do not know what they are doing" (Luke 23:34)?

NOTES

1. James D. Nogalski, *The Book of the Twelve: Hosea–Jonah*, Smyth & Helwys Bible Commentary (Macon GA: Smyth & Helwys, 2011) 445.

2. James Bruckner, *Jonah, Nahum, Habakkuk, Zephaniah*, The NIV Application Commentary (Grand Rapids MI: Zondervan, 2004) 110–11.

3. Jack M. Sasson, *Jonah*, The Anchor Bible (New York: Doubleday, 1990) 282.

4. James Limburg, *Jonah*, The Old Testament Library (Louisville KY: Westminster/John Knox, 1993) 93.

5. Ibid., 95.

6. Sasson, *Jonah*, 298.

7. Douglas Stuart, *Hosea–Jonah*, Word Biblical Commentary (Grand Rapids MI: Zondervan, 1988) 505.

8. Sasson, *Jonah*, 307.

9. Limburg, *Jonah*, 97.

10. Ibid.

11. Terence E. Fretheim, *The Message of Jonah* (Minneapolis: Augsburg, 1977) 24.

12. Simon Wiesenthal, *The Sunflower*, rev. and exp. ed. (New York: Schocken, 1997).

13. For an insightful commentary on how Jonah applies to the reconciliation of victims and oppressors, see Miguel A. De La Torre, *Liberating Jonah: Forming an Ethics of Reconciliation* (Maryknoll NY: Orbis, 2007).

14. Miroslav Volf, *Exclusion and Embrace* (Nashville: Abingdon, 1996) 116.

15. Leif Enger, *Peace Like a River* (New York: Atlantic Monthly, 2001) 79–80.

TEACHING JONAH
TO YOUTH

Introduction

Many students will be familiar with the story of Jonah. Their parents and teachers likely told them the story of Jonah and the fish. Popular retellings of the Jonah story, like *Jonah: A Veggie Tales Movie,* may shape their understanding of the story far more than the biblical text does. The following lessons attempt to increase the students' understanding of the biblical account. They also help teenagers explore the author's use of irony and exaggeration to convey the theological assertions of the story. Finally, the lessons seek to equip students to apply these theological themes to their lives.

When students base their understanding of Jonah's story solely on popular retellings or childhood memories, they often miss the point of the story. They view Jonah's time in the belly of the fish as a punishment rather than salvation. They see the moral of the story as similar to the lesson of many proverbs: obey God and good things will happen to you; disobey God and suffer the consequences. While one can find that lesson in the book of Jonah, the book also contains far more interesting issues concerning the interchange between mercy and judgment. These more complex issues drive the conflict between Jonah and his God.

Moralizing tends to make a biblical story less appealing, but the more challenging issues of when and how to apply mercy and judgment have the potential to connect with students in a meaningful way. Teenagers live in a world in which issues of injustice dominate the headlines. Terrorist groups delight in evil much like the ancient Assyrians did. Multinational corporations maximize profits over the welfare of the environment and the poor. In our culture, individuals rape, murder, and harm others without regard for the damage they do. Students recognize this is the world they are inheriting. They have a strong desire to see the world set right and to participate in that process.

The book of Jonah engages students' desires to see the world set right. It also introduces them to important questions. How will God set the world right? Will God punish evildoers or will they be shown mercy? Should we care about oppressors in the same way we care about victims? Do we want to live in a world in which the worst of the bad guys seemingly get a "pass"? Would we be willing to be agents of God's good news if God required us to take that good news to our sworn enemies?

I encourage the students to read the text closely. There they will discover a thoroughly entertaining story that also challenges our notions of justice, mercy, and the breadth of God's concern. My hope is that when students engage both the text and the questions it raises, their love of the biblical text will grow. Jonah is far more than a children's story. It is a challenging parable for our day and age. As such, the book of Jonah can serve as an entry point for our students to develop their appreciation for the relevance of the biblical text in the world today.

Session Outline
Session 1: God Calls and Jonah Flees (1:1-16)
Session 2: Jonah Prays and God Saves (1:17–2:10)
Session 3: Jonah Preaches and Nineveh Repents (3:1-10)
Session 4: Jonah Questions and God Responds (4:1-11)

GOD CALLS AND JONAH FLEES

Jonah 1:1-16

Supplies: Map of Jonah's world posted in the classroom for reference; white board and markers; copies of Jonah 1:1-16; pictures or action figures of popular superheroes and villains

WELCOME

Each week, welcome students into your classroom. Invite them to share about their week, being sensitive to youth who are more reserved. Ask specific questions and follow up in the coming weeks.

OPENING ACTIVITY: HEROES, HEROINES, AND VILLAINS

Begin by drawing two columns on the board. Label one column "Heroes/Heroines." Label the other column "Villains." Ask the students to name some of their favorite movie villains. Then ask the students to name their favorite movie heroes or heroines. Share with the students how directors dress characters in specific ways to alert us as to whether that person is good or bad. For example, in old Westerns, the good guy often wore a white hat, while the bad guy often wore a black one. Ask, "What are other ways directors indicate who the good guys are versus who the bad guys are?" Then ask, "Can you think of any movies in which the director plays on these stereotypes?" Invite the students to discuss why a movie might present the hero/heroine and the villain in unconventional ways (for example, the hero is bland while the villain is charming).

Explain that in the book of Jonah, the author plays against our expectations. In the Hebrew Scriptures, prophets often play the role of hero or heroine. They denounce injustice and defend the poor and defenseless against the oppression of the powerful. Non-Jews often fill the role of villains in the Hebrew Scriptures, and perhaps no villain is as evil as the Assyrians. First, they are not Israelites, which means they worship foreign gods. The Assyrians also delight in doing evil. By the end of the book, though, Jonah will be anything but a hero, and the Assyrians in Nineveh will act in unexpected ways. Ask the students, "Why do you think the author might tell the story in this way?"

STUDY THE SCRIPTURE: JONAH 1:1-16

Split the class into two groups. Give each group a copy of Jonah 1:1-16. Translations like the Common English Bible or the English Standard Version work best for this exercise. Ask one group to read the verses and identify any words that appear more than once. Have the second group read the verses and identify all the characters in the story.

When they finish reading, invite the first group of students to share which words they found repeated in chapter 1 (*great, evil, get up, down, hurl,* and *terrified*). Explain that the book of Jonah was originally meant to be heard and not read. The repetition of words helped the original hearers both remember the story and pick out what was important. Challenge the youth to pay attention to this repetition of phrases throughout the book.

Invite the second group of students to share the different characters who appear in Jonah 1:1-16. List the characters on the board. Ask the class if they think the original audience would have thought each character was a hero, a villain, or something in between. Draw from the material in the introduction and session 1 of the Jonah ABS Teaching Guide to elaborate on the ancient expectations of prophets, Assyrians, and sailors.

Next, ask volunteers to read through the text in four sections: Jonah 1:1-3; Jonah 1:4-6; Jonah 1:7-12; and Jonah 1:13-16. After reading each portion of the Scripture, explore with the class their expectations of the characters versus how the characters actually behave.

Ask, "Why do you think the sailors responded to God with prayer and worship?"

After discussion, ask, "Why do you think Jonah reacted to God by running away? How is submitting to being thrown in the sea another attempt to run away? What else might Jonah have done?"

MAKING CONNECTIONS

Discuss with the class the following questions.

1. Why do believers sometimes run from God's call?
2. What are some modern examples of situations where unbelievers seem more in tune with what God is doing in the world than believers?
3. How does the story of Jonah, with its reversals of expectations, connect with what we know of Jesus' story in the New Testament?
4. What lessons does Jonah's story in Jonah 1:1-16 have for the church today?

CLOSING ACTIVITY

Point to the collection of superhero/villain action figures or pictures. Ask the students who each one is and what he or she is known for. Ask, "If you could be any one of these characters, who would you choose and why?" Then guide the students to think of "heroes" they know personally. Ask questions like these.

• What did/does this person do to make him or her a hero in your opinion?
• How do you think God feels about real-life heroes and villains, and how should you treat these people?
• How can you be a "hero" in someone's life?

PRAY

Close the session with prayer. Either invite students to pray, or say your own prayer, asking that God would help us recognize that we all have the potential to be heroes and villains. Pray for God's direction as we interact with others.

JONAH PRAYS AND GOD SAVES

Jonah 1:17–2:10

Supplies: Two whiteboards or two flip charts, markers, white paper, timer, colors or colored pencils, recording of the song "Mighty to Save" by Hillsong (check YouTube)

WELCOME

Welcome students into your classroom. Ask if anyone wants to share about a "heroic" deed they witnessed the past week.

OPENING ACTIVITY: PICTIONARY

Before the lesson, prepare two sets of cards for a game of Pictionary. Include the following words in each set: *life jacket, life preserver ring, float, lifeguard, motorboat, sailboat, helicopter, rope, pool noodle, surfboard, paddleboat, Jet Ski.* When class begins, divide the students into two teams. Have each team nominate a person who will draw. Provide each team with a marker, a set of cards, and a whiteboard or flip chart. Have the teams compete at the same time. Set a timer for two minutes. The team that completes the most correct guesses wins.

After the game, invite the teams to guess what the various cards have in common. (They can all be used to rescue someone who is drowning.) Ask, "Which objects would be the most helpful form of rescue in a pool? In a lake? In the ocean?"

Ask if anyone has ever been rescued from a dangerous situation. If so, how did they feel after being rescued? If not, how do students think they would feel after being rescued from a life-threatening situation? Explain that God used an unconventional means, a great fish, to rescue Jonah as Jonah was sinking in the sea.

STUDY THE SCRIPTURES: JONAH 1:17–2:10

Remind the students of how the author of Jonah repeats keywords and phrases. Have the students read Jonah 1:17–2:10 silently, looking for some of the keywords that have already shown up in the book. Encourage them to share what they discover.

Ask the students if they remember what Jonah was doing at the end of last week's session. Take a moment to explain that ancient Jews feared the sea. To be tossed into the sea was to invite certain death. As Jonah sank, God intervened. Invite a student to read Jonah 1:17 and 2:10 aloud. Explain that these two verses carry the action of the story. Between the fish swallowing Jonah and vomiting him up on dry land, Jonah offers a prayer to the Lord. In the words of that prayer, we discover what happened to Jonah as he was sinking to the depths of the sea.

At this point, students may question whether or not a person could survive being swallowed by a fish. If so, this may be the appropriate time to discuss the different views concerning the historicity of the story. Draw on the introduction to the Jonah ABS Teaching Guide to direct your discussion. As interesting as this topic will be for the students, try not to spend too much time on the issue. Help the students understand that whether or not the story is to be taken literally, the main themes of the book remain applicable for our lives today. For instance, when we cry out to God for help, God delights in rescuing us.

Next, move through the story together, verse by verse.

Invite a student to read Jonah 2:1-2 aloud. Ask the students, "What do these verses say that Jonah did? How is this different from Jonah's actions in the first chapter? What do you think made the difference?" Then ask the students, "How did God respond? Why do you think God rescued Jonah?"

Invite a student to read Jonah 2:3-4 aloud. Ask, "Who does Jonah say hurled him into the sea?" Discuss the reasons Jonah may attribute his flight into the sea to God's hand. Talk with the students about how what appears as a punishment might be a form of salvation. Jonah tried to run from God, but God intervened by bringing a storm. This storm led to Jonah being tossed into the sea. Drowning proved distressing to Jonah, but his distress caused him to seek the very God from whom he was running. Ask the students, "When has distress caused you to turn to God?"

Invite a student to read Jonah 2:4-7 aloud. Ask the students to list the terms that refer to the threat of drowning. Explain that many of these words had a double meaning for ancient Jews. These words could apply to both the depths of the ocean and Sheol, the place of the dead. Jonah was sinking to the bottom of the ocean and drawing near to death. Only as his life "was ebbing away" did Jonah offer a prayer to God. Ask the students, "Why do we sometimes wait until the last minute to ask God for help? What does it say about us that we put God off until it is almost too late? What does it say about God that God forgives us even then?"

Invite a student to read Jonah 2:8-9 aloud. Explain that Jonah's words follow the traditional form of a thanksgiving psalm. Discuss how the phrase, "Deliverance belongs to the LORD," serves as a conclusion for Jonah's psalm but also as foreshadowing of what is to come. How might Jonah's words come back to haunt him?

MAKING CONNECTIONS

Discuss the following questions together.
• How would you have felt in Jonah's position?
• Have you ever gotten what you knew you deserved? If so, what was that like?
• Has God ever helped you during a situation when you knew you had made a mistake and would suffer the consequences? If so, what was that like?
• What do you think Jonah will do next?

CLOSING ACTIVITY

Explain how the story of Jonah and the fish has inspired countless artists to paint, draw, and sculpt the prophet and the sea creature. Distribute art supplies, and invite the students to draw a picture of Jonah inside the belly of a fish. Have them label the depths of the sea with things that cause them distress or threaten to overwhelm them. Invite the students to write a prayer for help on the back of their drawings. If they prefer, they may write a psalm of thanksgiving for a time when God delivered them from a difficult situation. Conclude by listening to or singing together the song "Mighty to Save."

PRAY

Close the session with prayer. Either invite students to pray, or say your own prayer, asking that God would help us realize when we are wrong. Pray for the strength to turn to God in such times and to do better.

JONAH PREACHES AND NINEVEH REPENTS

Jonah 3:1-10

WELCOME

Welcome students into your classroom. Ask if anyone wants to share briefly about a way that God rescued them the past week.

OPENING ACTIVITY: SERMON IN A SENTENCE

Talk with the students about how the social media site Twitter works. If they do not already know, explain that tweets (statements posted on Twitter) are limited to just 140 characters. Ask them if they think they could construct a sermon using only 140 characters or less. You might encourage them to use the hashtag #sermoninasentence to find actual examples online. If your Bible study occurs after your pastor has preached, you may want to challenge the students to condense the pastor's sermon into a sentence or two.

Next, challenge the students to come up with their own sentence-length sermons for various topics. Can they write a Christmas sermon in a sentence? What about an Easter sermon? How might they turn the story of Jonah into a sermon in a sentence? Hand out supplies, and have them write their attempts on sheets of paper. Invite the students to share their sermons. Ask, "What do you think about the possibility of our pastor preaching one-sentence sermons?

What would happen? What would be the advantages of one-sentence sermons? What might go wrong?"

Tell them that when Jonah finally reached Nineveh, he preached a one-sentence sermon. Note that in the Hebrew, Jonah's sermon contained only five words. His sermon was short even for a tweet! Nevertheless, his short sermon had a big impact, leading to the conversion of the entire city of Nineveh.

STUDY THE SCRIPTURES: JONAH 3:1-10

Remind the students again that the author of Jonah likes to repeat keywords and phrases. Have the students read Jonah 3:1-10 silently while looking for some of the keywords that have already shown up in the book. Encourage them to share what they discover. Then work through the text together, verse by verse

Invite a student to read Jonah 3:1-3 aloud. Ask the students if this passage reminds them of anything. Invite a student to reread Jonah 1:1-3 aloud for the class. Then ask the students to discuss the differences. Ask, "When have you messed up but received a second chance? How did receiving a second chance make you feel? How did receiving a second chance change your behavior or actions the second time around?"

Invite a student to read aloud Jonah 3:4-5. Guide the students to critique Jonah's sermon. Ask, "What do you notice about the sermon? Is the sermon missing anything important? How might you have preached it differently?" Ask the group to think about Jonah's reasons for preaching the sermon in this way. Do they think he preached his sermon with a good attitude or a bad one? Explore the reasons a preacher might purposefully preach a bad sermon.

Ask the students to think about how people would respond today if someone preached a similar sermon throughout the streets of their city. How did the Ninevites respond? Take this opportunity to talk about repentance. Explain what repentance is and why it is necessary for the life of faith. Talk about how sackcloth served as a sign of repentance in ancient times. Ask the students, "What might serve as an outward sign of repentance for us today?"

Invite another student to read aloud Jonah 3:6-9. Ask the students to evaluate this scene. Do they think the scene is supposed to be read dramatically or as comedy? Ask them to explain their choice. Tell them that the author of Jonah often describes situations that appear outlandish for the purpose of making a serious theological point. The scene with the king of Nineveh may be one of those moments. While kings are supposed to lead their people into important decisions, this king follows his people's lead. To make up for lost time, he makes the animals participate in public forms of repentance just like the people. Nevertheless, this goofy king makes some important theological points. Ask, "What does the king say the people must repent or turn away from? What does the king hope God will do as a result of their repentance? Why does the king say that God *might* relent instead of promising that God *will* relent from sending punishment?" Discuss the difference between God being *willing* to forgive us and God *having* to forgive us.

Invite a student to read Jonah 3:10 aloud. Ask, "What does this verse teach us about God? Do you think God is capable of changing God's mind?" Invite the students to explain their thoughts. Then ask, "Does the image of God we get in the book of Jonah match the image of God we get in other parts of the Bible? How does this picture of God compare with other texts? How does it contrast with other texts?" (Be ready to help the students if they struggle to answer these questions. You might look up some example texts beforehand. For the idea that God is always the same, see Mal 3:6; Num 23:19; 1 Sam 15:29; Ps 33:11; Jas 1:17; Heb 13:8. For the idea that God can change, see Exod 32:14; Jer 18:8; 26:19; Amos 7:3, 6; 2 Sam 24:16).

MAKING CONNECTIONS

Remind the students that this section of Jonah begins and ends with God granting a second chance. First, God gave Jonah a second chance to preach to the Ninevites. Second, God gave the Ninevites a second chance at life after they repented from their sins. Discuss these questions together.

• If you feel comfortable, share some areas of your lives in which you might need a second chance. (As the leader, you can facilitate this conversation by sharing your own story. Be sure never to pressure teenagers to share sensitive information in front of the group. Do let them know that you and other trusted adults are available if they wish to speak more privately.)
• What is grace? Do you think God showed grace to any of the characters in this story? If so, to whom and how?

• What is the difference between seeking God's forgiveness and presuming upon God's grace?

CLOSING ACTIVITY

Distribute paper and pens. As the students feel comfortable, encourage them to write about situations, sins, or other areas of their lives where they may need a second chance. They can list things, draw pictures, or write brief journal entries. Then, if they wish, they can tear up the papers and put them in a trash can. This shows that, when we repent of our wrongs, God always gives us a second chance and forgets our sins. If desired, you can play a recording of the Casting Crowns song "East to West" about God's forgiveness.

PRAY

Close the session with prayer. Either invite students to pray, or say your own prayer, thanking God for second chances. Ask God to help us to seek forgiveness when we should and then to move forward in grace.

JONAH QUESTIONS AND GOD RESPONDS

Jonah 4:1-11

Supplies: Newspapers and/or news magazines, paper, pens

OPENING ACTIVITY: SETTING THE WORLD RIGHT

Give the students time to look through the newspapers and news magazines. Ask them to look for examples of humans behaving badly. After they have sufficient time to locate examples, invite the students to share with the group the examples they found. Ask the students, "If you were in a position of power and could exert change in these situations, how would you respond? Would you punish the evildoers? If the evildoers said they were sorry, would you forgive them? Why or why not?" Discuss how the victims of these bad examples might feel if their oppressors were forgiven instead of punished. (Be aware that, for some students, the exploration of tragic world events might be unsettling, especially if the student is a victim of violence or abuse. Be sensitive to the needs of your students and adjust accordingly.)

Explain that Jonah's protest in chapter 4 surfaces from his questions about the perceived need to balance mercy with justice. While Jonah was glad to receive God's mercy in chapter 2, he feels as if God's forgiveness of the Ninevites goes too far.

STUDY THE SCRIPTURES: JONAH 4:1-11

In this last week of the study, remind the students once more about the author of Jonah's repetition of keywords and phrases. Have the students read Jonah 4:1-11 silently while looking for some of the keywords that have already shown up in the book. Also challenge them to notice words that repeat only within this passage. Encourage them to share what they discover. Next, move through the passage together, verse by verse.

Invite a student to read Jonah 4:1-4 aloud. Ask the students to explain in their own words why Jonah is angry with God. Ask, "Have you ever been angry that someone did not get in trouble for doing something wrong?" Revisit some of the atrocities committed by the Assyrians noted in the introduction of the Jonah ABS Teaching Guide. Ask, "Do you think Jonah had a right to be angry with God?" Encourage them to explain their reasoning.

Invite a student to read Jonah 4:5-8 aloud. Explain that scholars are not quite sure why Jonah went out and sat on the hill. Some scholars think Jonah was hoping God would change his mind. Those writers also think Jonah may have understood the arrival of the miraculous growing plant as a sign that God had come around to Jonah's way of thinking. Ask, "Do you ever try to convince God to do things your way?"

Then ask the students to explain in their own words what happened next. Point out that God sends or appoints the plant, the worm, and the scorching east wind just as God sent or appointed the fish in chapter 2. In each case, God provided or appointed something from nature to intervene in Jonah's life. In chapter 2, God provided the fish as a means of salvation. Ask the students, "Do you think God provided the plant, worm, and wind in chapter 4 as a punishment or as a form of deliverance?" Discuss their various viewpoints. Ask, "How did Jonah view them?"

Invite a student to read Jonah 4:9-11. Note that God has asked Jonah a second time whether or not he has a right to be angry with God. The first time, Jonah ignored God's question. This time, he asserts his right to be angry. God then responds with a justification for the mercy shown to the Ninevites. Ask the students to explain God's reasons for forgiving the Ninevites.

God points out that Jonah felt concern and sorrow for the loss of the plant. Ask the students whether they would grieve the loss of a pet. Explain that God's words convey the idea that God would feel Nineveh's destruction as a loss. Ask, "Would you grieve the deaths of those who did the terrible things that we read about in the newspapers? Do you think God would grieve their deaths and damnation?" Discuss why God may grieve the deaths of those we view as evil.

MAKING CONNECTIONS

Invite a student to read aloud Jonah 4:12. Note that there is no Jonah 4:12! Ask, "Do you think this is a good place to end the story? Why do you think the author ended the story here? How do you think Jonah responded to God? How might we respond to God if we were in a similar situation?"

Invite a student to read aloud Matthew 5:43-48. Ask the group to think of people we might label as enemies. Discuss what it might look like for God to show mercy to these people. Discuss how it would make us feel if God acted mercifully toward our enemies.

CLOSING ACTIVITY

Invite the group to write or act out a more complete ending to Jonah's story. They can work separately or in small groups as desired. Give them time to complete their stories or prepare their skits, and then allow them to share the results with the class. Ask questions like these.

• What do you think is the best ending to Jonah's story?

• If there are times when you have run away from God or only done enough as little as possible of what God asks of you, how did your story end?

• What would be a better ending for that story in your life?

• What changes can you make so that your next story has a happier ending?

PRAY

Close the session with prayer. Either invite students to pray, or say your own prayer, thanking God for the example of Jonah, who acted in ways that are very human. Thank God for the grace shown to Jonah and to us.

TEACHING JONAH
TO CHILDREN

Introduction

As I read through the book of Jonah and the Smyth & Helwys Commentary on it, I was reminded again of how much God loves us. Jonah refuses God, tries to run away to the end of the world as he knows it, gets swallowed by a fish, finally begs God to save him after three days, goes to Nineveh against his will, says five words (in Hebrew) to the people of Nineveh and gives them no hope, sulks because God doesn't destroy them, and begs to die. He does all of that, yet God still loves him. God patiently waits for Jonah to figure out God's compassion, to realize that he is a recipient of that compassion as well, and to discover that other people deserve the same compassion.

Jonah is a book of unexpected happenings. We don't expect God's prophet to run away from God's call. We don't expect the sailors to throw Jonah into the sea even if that's the only way to stop the storm. We don't expect the sailors to turn to God and believe. We don't expect the fish to save Jonah. We expect Jonah to go to Nineveh eventually, but we don't expect him to be so rude when he prophesies to the people there. Finally, we don't expect the Ninevites to realize how wrong they have been and to show remorse. While we may not expect any of that, we, like Jonah, expect God to show compassion. Jonah ran because, as it says in Jonah 4:2, he knew that God was "a merciful and compassionate God, very patient, full of faithful love, and willing not to destroy." He

Jessica Asbell is currently serving as the minister to children at First Baptist Church of Roswell, Georgiga. She has worked with children in various capacities at several churches, including Winter Park Baptist in Wilmington, North Carolina; First Baptist of Decatur, Georgia; and Highland Hills Baptist in Macon, Georgia. She has a Master of Divinity from McAfee School of Theology and a BBA from Mercer University. In her spare time she loves to read, watch movies, and spend time with her sweet kitty, Lucy.

knew that God was compassionate and that God would save the city. Jonah didn't want the city to be saved, so he ran away.

Lest we judge Jonah too harshly, we should recognize that there are times when we do the same thing. We don't like some people in this world. It may be because they have done something to hurt us in some way or because, based on our laws and our morality, we view them as terrible people. It is hard, for instance, for us to like murderers. Terrorists. ISIS. It is hard for us to like people who have done horrific things. Imagine with me that God has asked you to go to ISIS and tell them to repent. Perhaps the Ninevites were nothing like ISIS, but perhaps they were. Maybe Jonah was running because he was xenophobic, or maybe he was running because he was afraid for his life. I don't know about you, but I believe that if God told me to give a message to ISIS, I'd run away too. Perhaps we give Jonah too much credit with this example, but might we, too, have difficulty following God's call to testify to certain people about repentance?

Each of these sessions on Jonah uses fun activities to help kids identify with Jonah's story. Before the session each week, read through all the options and decide which ones will work best with your group and gather the needed materials. Every session includes a simple telling of the story along with activities to help children understand it. You can also help them learn a memory verse and offer snacks. **If you plan to serve the snack options, be sure to check for food allergies first.**

Remember that children are active. If you notice your group getting bored or fidgety, be ready to move to another activity. It's also helpful to include time for kids to stand up and stretch, do jumping jacks, run in place, and do other fun movements that help them get their "wiggles" out before you try to discuss the stories with them.

The first session, "You Can't Outrun God," centers on Jonah 1:1-16. Jonah realizes that no matter how far he runs, he can't get away from God. He tries and tries, but he merely ends up with a mouthful of seawater, smelling like a fish. By playing hide and seek, preschoolers will learn that we can't hide from something we don't want to do, and we can't hide from God. By attempting a list of "impossible" things, elementary-aged children will learn that running away and hiding from God is impossible. Children will also learn just how far Tarshish was from Nineveh (2,600 miles!) and what that means in distance for us. They will use situation cards to help them see that they have a choice just like Jonah did.

In "Save Me!"—the second session—the children study the story of Jonah in the belly of the fish (1:17–2:10). Your group will have the chance to use their noses and determine what smells good and what smells bad, a physical reminder that it was smelly in the belly of the fish. They will talk about times when they, like Jonah, have been angry with someone for telling them to do something they didn't want to do. The children will also talk about songs of thanksgiving. Preschoolers will draw a picture of a song of thanksgiving, younger school-aged children will use the worksheet at the end of the lesson to write a song of thanksgiving, and older children will write their own songs.

The third session, "They Listened," is based on Jonah finally going to Nineveh in Jonah 3:1-10. In this story, the Ninevites listen to Jonah and show remorse—just as he feared they would. In the opening activity, children will play a version of Red Rover that helps them realize how Jonah tried to make it hard for the Ninevites to be saved. God uses people who make mistakes, and God also does things that we don't always expect. For reflection time, preschoolers will play a game to understand that God can save anyone. Younger school-aged children will talk about the unexpected and surprising things God has done in their lives, and older children will list their sins on paper, ask God for forgiveness, tear the papers up, and throw them in the trash to symbolize that God chooses to forget our sins.

The final session—"You Forgave Them?"—focuses on Jonah's reaction to God's compassion. In Jonah 4:1-11, we see that Jonah has a sour attitude. He isn't happy that God saved Nineveh, and he actually climbs a hill to sit and wait for God to change the course of action. The opening activity for this session involves planting flowers. Each child will plant a flower to help them remember that God sent a plant to Jonah for shade. After they explore the Bible story, you'll guide them to talk about times when it's hard to forgive someone. In session 3 they asked for forgiveness, and in session 4 they will learn to forgive others.

While each session contains options for children of various ages, feel free to modify them as needed to suit your group. Through these sessions, it is my hope that children will see that they cannot hide from God, that God uses people who make mistakes, that God is always willing to forgive, and that we can forgive others even when it's hard.

Session Outline

Session 1: You Can't Outrun God (1:1-16)

Session 2: Save Me! (1:17–2:10)

Session 3: They Listened (3:1-10)

Session 4: You Forgave Them? (4:1-11)

YOU CAN'T OUTRUN GOD

Jonah 1:1-16

BEFORE THE SESSION

Read through the activities. Gather and/or prepare materials for the ones you choose. Become familiar with the Bible story.

WELCOME

Greet children with a smile and a welcome as they come into your classroom. Make sure they know that you're happy to be there with them!

OPENING ACTIVITY: HIDE AND SEEK/IMPOSSIBLE FEATS

For Preschoolers

Play a few rounds of hide and seek (and make sure everyone is found each time). Then talk about the game.

• Was it hard to find a good hiding place?
• Was it hard to find those who were hiding?

Explain that it might have taken a few minutes and a little help, but we found everyone each time. Sometimes we think we can hide when we don't want to do something. But our parents or someone else always finds us. In the Bible story today, Jonah doesn't want to do something. He tries to run and hide from God. Do the children think Jonah could hide from God?

FOR SCHOOL-AGED CHILDREN

Challenge the children to attempt the following feats.
• Touch your nose or chin with your tongue.
• Tickle yourself.
• Put your whole fist in your mouth.
• Sit down, then lift your right foot off the floor and make clockwise circles. Continue doing this and try to trace the number "6" in the air with your finger. (The number "6" includes a counter-clockwise circle, so their feet will likely switch direction.)
• Raise one eyebrow without moving the other as well.
• Lick your elbow.
• Wiggle your ears.

Talk about the activity. Was anyone able to do the "impossible feats"? Explain that this is actually a list of things that are impossible to do. No matter how hard we try, we'll never be able to do these things exactly as listed. Tell the group that in our Bible story today, Jonah tries to run away and hide from God. Do they think Jonah could hide from God?

THE BIBLE STORY: YOU CAN'T OUTRUN GOD

Read Jonah 1:1-16 from an easy-to-understand translation like the Contemporary English Version (CEV), the Common English Bible (CEB), or a Bible storybook with pictures. Then explain that God told Jonah to go to Nineveh, which was about 500 miles away. Instead, Jonah tried to run away to Tarshish, which seemed like the edge of the world to him and was about 2,000 miles away. Strange things happened on Jonah's journey.

Now read the story again as follows, but ask the children to act it out as you read. Help them decide who will be God, Jonah, the sailors, the officer, and stagehands who handle props. You can give them cues as suggested in parentheses. Also encourage them to use the props you brought. Before the story starts, they might arrange a group of chairs and boxes to serve as a ship with cargo. Have the sheet nearby to represent the sea.

God told Jonah, "Get up and go to Nineveh. Tell the people that I have seen the wrong things they are doing." Jonah got up (Jonah stands), *but he decided to run away from God to a place called Tarshish.* (Jonah runs) *At Jaffa, he got on a ship that was going to Tarshish.* (Sailors have a ship made of chairs, and Jonah sits with them.) *While they were on the sea, God sent a great wind and storm.* (Stage-hands move the sheet up and down like waves.) *It looked like the ship would break and sink. The sailors were terrified.* (Sailors look scared.) *Each one cried out to his god. They also threw the ship's cargo overboard to make it lighter.* (Sailors toss boxes off the chairs.) *Guess where Jonah was? Inside the ship asleep!* (Jonah lies down among the chairs and pretends to sleep.) *The ship's officer found him and said, "How can you sleep at a time like this? Get up and ask your god to save us!"* (Officer stands by Jonah and shakes him awake.) *The other sailors tried to figure out why the storm happened. They saw that it was Jonah's fault.* (Sailors approach Jonah.) *They said to him, "You are the reason for this storm. What do you do? Where are you from?" Jonah said, "I'm a Hebrew. I worship the God of heaven who made the sea and the dry land." The sailors were even more scared.* (Sailors look terrified! The sea is still full of angry waves.) *"What have you done?" they asked. "How can we calm the sea?" Jonah told them, "Pick me up and throw me into the sea! That will make it calm. I know this is my fault." The sailors tried to row to land.* (Sailors pretend to row.) *The sea was too rough. So they said to Jonah's God, "Please don't let us die because of Jonah! You are the Lord. You can do whatever you want." Then they picked up Jonah and threw him into the sea.* (Sailors pretend to do this. Jonah lies back down and rolls onto the sheet. All is calm.) *When the sea grew calm, the sailors worshiped God.* (Sailors kneel in prayer or raise their hands to heaven.)

Be sure to compliment the children on working together to act out the Bible story. Then ask them what it was like to pretend to be the different characters. Did it help them understand the story better?

RESPONDING: HOW FAR DID JONAH RUN?

Before the Session: Find a world map or globe to bring to class. Look up the distances between several cities in your state and be ready to share these with the children. Explain that God told Jonah to go to Nineveh, which is in modern-day Iraq. Instead, Jonah got on a boat headed to Tarshish, which is in Spain. Use the map or globe to show the distance between the two places. They are 2,641 miles apart. To help the children understand this distance, ask them if they think the following pairs of cities are closer together or further apart than Nineveh and Tarshish: Atlanta and New York (862 miles), London and Paris (295 miles), Atlanta and San Francisco (2,473 miles), and cities in your state. After the children answer each time, point to the two cities on the map or globe and tell them the true distance. Note that all of these cities are closer together than Nineveh and Tarshish.

Now tell the group about Interstate 40, a long road that goes from the Atlantic Ocean on the East Coast to the Pacific Ocean on the West Coast. Using the map or globe, tell them it begins in Wilmington, North Carolina, and ends in Barstow, California. Do they think this road is longer or shorter than the distance between Nineveh and Tarshish? Then explain that this road is about 2,889 miles. So it's a little farther than the distance between Nineveh and Tarshish, but not much! It's as if Jonah tried to travel across the whole United States to run away from what God wanted him to do. He wanted to get as far away as he could, but he couldn't outrun or hide from God. God is *always* with us, no matter where we are. Close this activity by reading Psalm 139:7-8 (CEB): "Where could I go to get away from your spirit? Where could I go to escape your presence? If I went up to heaven, you would be there. If I went down to the grave, you would be there too!"

ALTERNATE OPTION: SITUATION CARDS

Before the Session: Make a copy of the "Situation Cards" (pg. 136) and cut them apart.

Explain that God asked Jonah to do something that he didn't want to do. Sometimes there are things we should do even though we may not want to do them. The situations on the cards could happen in our everyday lives. Divide the children into groups and give each group a situation card. You could also read each situation to the whole group and ask what they would do for each one. Close the activity with a brief discussion using questions like these: Why would you make this choice? How would it help? Would your decision please God?

SNACK TIME

Before the Session: Prepare grapes, almonds, and crackers. Bring cups for water.
Explain that in ancient times, sailors ate foods like almonds, grapes, figs, and pomegranates. They also drank wine because they didn't have much clean water. Many times they had to fish if they wanted to eat meat. For our snack today, we will eat some of the things sailors would have eaten.

Say a prayer of thanks together, and then provide grapes, almonds, crackers, and water. As the children eat, talk about how today's sailors have refrigerators, freezers, and even ovens on their boats. They can eat lots of different foods just like us. But in Jonah's time, they had to take what could be packed in crates and not spoil.

MEMORY VERSE ACTIVITY: OVERBOARD!

Before the Session: Make copies of the "Overboard" worksheet (pg. 137).
Memory Verse: "I worship the LORD, the God of heaven—who made the sea and the dry land." (Jonah 1:9)

Remind the group that Jonah was thrown overboard into the sea. Tell them to pretend that our Bible verse got mixed up when he landed in the ocean. Can they unscramble the letters to see what it says? Hand out copies of the worksheet and encourage them to work together if needed.

For nonreaders, write the memory verse at the top of a piece of white paper or construction paper for each child. Have the children draw pictures of the land and sea as you all practice saying the verse.

CLOSING PRAYER

God, thank you that it is impossible for us to hide from you. You love us enough to find us no matter where we go. Please give us courage to do the things you ask us to do, even when we don't want to. Amen.

SITUATION CARDS

Session 1

Make a copy of this page, then cut out the cards on the dotted lines.

- -

Situation 1

Imagine you see the new kid at school eating lunch by herself. You know you should go sit with her, but your friends are sitting on the other side of the cafeteria. What do you do?

- -

Situation 2

A bully at school keeps making fun of you. One day you see that bully sitting by himself on a bench. He looks sad about something. What do you do?

- -

Situation 3

Your mom makes you invite a certain kid to your birthday party every year. This year she forgot to remind you. Do you invite the kid or not? Why?

- -

Situation 4

A new family moved in next door. They have children about your age, but the kids look different from you and go to a mosque instead of a church like yours. You see them outside one day. Do you go play with them?

- -

Situation 5

You're going to play soccer with your friends. Your younger brother or sister wants to go along. You know he or she isn't a good player. What do you do?

- -

Situation 6

You're in gym class and are chosen to be team captain for a game. You want all your friends on your team, but suddenly you see the kid who is always picked last. He looks sad, like he knows he will be picked last again. What do you do?

BIBLE VERSE WORKSHEET: OVERBOARD!

Session 1

Jonah went overboard and our Bible verse got all mixed up! The letters are confused. The Zs have become As and the As have become Zs. Use this code to help you figure out the Bible verse.

A	B	C	D	E	F	G	H	I	J	K	L	M
Z	Y	X	W	V	U	T	S	R	Q	P	O	N

N	O	P	Q	R	S	T	U	V	W	X	Y	Z
M	L	K	J	I	H	G	F	E	D	C	B	A

"R dlihsrk gsv Oliw, gsv Tlw lu svzevm—dsl nzwv gsv hvz zmw gsv wib ozmw." Jonah 1:9

"

_____

_____

_____." (Jonah 1:9)

SAVE ME!

Jonah 1:17–2:10

BEFORE THE SESSION

Read through the activities. Gather and/or prepare materials for the ones you choose. Become familiar with the Bible story.

WELCOME

Greet children with a smile and a welcome as they come into your classroom. Make sure they know that you're happy to be there with them!

OPENING ACTIVITY: WHAT'S THAT SMELL?

Before the Session: Gather items that smell good, such as laundry detergent, shampoo, sweet spices, and marshmallow fluff, along with items that don't smell as good, like pickles, gym shoes, tuna, old oatmeal. Be as creative as you like. Place the items in a bag so the kids can't see them.

Remind the children that, last week, we learned that God wanted Jonah to go to Nineveh and tell the people to stop doing wrong. Instead, Jonah tried to run away to Tarshish. He got on a boat and they set sail. Then a huge storm came up and the sailors were terrified. Jonah told them the storm was his fault and asked them to throw him overboard. They did! This week, we're going to find out that God sent a big fish to swallow Jonah and save him from drowning. What do the children think it was like inside the fish's belly? Ask them to close their eyes for at least thirty seconds. Next, ask what it felt like to be in the darkness. Explain that it was very dark inside the fish, and Jonah was in there for more than thirty seconds. He was in there for three whole days!

Ask the children if they can imagine what it smelled like inside the fish. Then invite them to close their eyes again while you wave different scents under their noses. Vary among the good and bad smells, and allow them to guess what each smell is. Then have them open their eyes and see what produced each smell.

Encourage them to listen as you tell the story about what happened to Jonah inside the fish.

THE BIBLE STORY: SAVE ME!

Read Jonah 1:17–2:10 from an easy-to-understand translation like the Contemporary English Version (CEV), the Common English Bible (CEB), or a Bible storybook with pictures. You can also paraphrase the story. The following passage is from the CEV. As you read, consider pausing at various places and asking the children if they can imagine what is happening.

The LORD sent a big fish to swallow Jonah, and Jonah was inside the fish for three days and three nights. From inside the fish, Jonah prayed to the Lord his God: "When I was in trouble, LORD, I prayed to you, and you listened to me. From deep in the world of the dead, I begged for your help, and you answered my prayer. You threw me down to the bottom of the sea. The water was churning all around; I was completely covered by your mighty waves. I thought I was swept away from your sight, never again to see your holy temple. I was almost drowned by the swirling waters that surrounded me. Seaweed had wrapped around my head. I had sunk down below the underwater mountains; I knew that forever, I would be a prisoner there. But, you, LORD God, rescued me from that pit. When my life was slipping away, I remembered you—and in your holy temple you heard my prayer. All who worship worthless idols turn from the God who offers them mercy. But with shouts of praise, I will offer a sacrifice to you, my LORD. I will keep my promise, because you are the one with power to save." The LORD commanded the fish to vomit up Jonah on the shore. And it did.

Ask the group what Jonah did when he was inside the fish. Why do they think he prayed to God?

RESPONDING: A SONG OF THANKSGIVING

Before the Session: Gather supplies for the age group you teach. For preschoolers: white paper, crayons, and markers. For younger school-aged children: copies of the "Song of Thanksgiving" worksheet at the end of this lesson, pencils, and crayons or markers. For older children: white paper, pencils, and crayons or markers.

Tell your group that when Jonah cried out to God, his prayer was in the form of a thanksgiving song. Songs of thanksgiving are in other parts of the Bible too. There are many songs of thanksgiving in the book of Psalms. All of these thanksgiving songs have similar parts. Some of them invite people to sing praises and give thanks to God. Many of them, like the one in Jonah 2, have verses that tell the person's story of danger and how God rescued them. They also include a promise to make a sacrifice to God. In Jonah's case, he promised to do what he said he would do. Some thanksgiving songs have a blessing and a request to God.

Invite the children to write (or draw) songs of thanksgiving. Guide them to write (or draw) about a time when God helped them. They can give as many details as they wish. The point is to praise God for helping them. They can also add a promise to do something they told God they would do, or simply a promise to listen to God. Finally, they can add their own prayer requests to the song. Direct your group as appropriate depending on their ages and skill levels. Give them time to complete their songs of thanksgiving, and then them to share their songs with the group if they wish.

SNACK TIME

Before the Session: Prepare blue Jell-O cups filled with Swedish fish. Alternately, bring goldfish crackers or even seaweed chips. Also bring cups for water.

Remind the kids that last week they ate foods the sailors would have eaten on their trip. This week, they can enjoy a snack that reminds them of fish. Say a prayer of thanksgiving together before they eat the snack.

MEMORY VERSE ACTIVITY: TELEPHONE

Memory Verse: "I called out to the LORD in my distress, and he answered me."
(Jonah 2:2)

Help the group play a few rounds of "telephone" with the memory verse. Have everyone sit in a circle. You start by whispering the memory verse in someone's ear, then they whisper it in the ear of the person beside them, and so on until the verse comes back to you. You say it aloud again. By this point, the verse is probably mixed up and funny! At the end of the game, tell the group that sometimes it seems like God doesn't hear our prayers, or they end get mixed up like our verse did in this game. But as this memory verse reminds us, God always hears us and always answers us in some way.

CLOSING PRAYER

Thank you, God, for always being there for us. Thank you for helping us through tough times. Please help us follow you and do what you want us to do. Amen.

SONG OF THANKSGIVING WORKSHEET

Session 2

Sing praises to God because _____

_____.

I know that God loves me because _____

_____.

God has always been there for me. I know God is with me
when _____.

God helped me by _____

_____,

and that made me feel _____

_____.

God, I promise that I will try to _____

_____.

I pray for _____

_____.

Thank You, God, for who you are! Amen.

THEY LISTENED

Jonah 3:1-10

BEFORE THE SESSION

Read through the activities. Gather and/or prepare materials for the ones you choose. Become familiar with the Bible story.

WELCOME

Greet children with a smile and a welcome as they come into your classroom. Make sure they know that you're happy to be there with them!

OPENING ACTIVITY: RED ROVER

Play the game "Red Rover" several times. Have the children make two lines at opposite ends of the room or outdoor space. Ask one line of kids to hold hands. Then have them say "Red Rover, Red Rover, send (name of a child) over." The object is for the child who is called to run and attempt to break through the linked hands of two kids in the opposite line. The first time, have the linked line try their hardest not to let anyone through. The second time, however, ask them secretly to let everyone through.

When the game is over, talk about it using questions like these: Was it hard to get through the line the first time? How about the second time? When I asked one team to let everyone through, how did you feel about making it so easy for the other team?

Remind the group that we've been learning about how God asked Jonah to go to Nineveh and tell the people to repent—to stop doing wrong and turn to God instead. But Jonah didn't go right away. Instead, he ran away from God.

He tried to go as far as he could, but he ended up in the belly of a fish. Finally, Jonah said a prayer inside the fish and said he would do what God wanted him to do. The fish spit him out and Jonah went to Nineveh. The problem is that he didn't really want the people to repent and turn back to God. He tried to make it very hard for them, but God wants *everyone* to stop doing wrong and turn back to God. What do you think happened next?

THE BIBLE STORY: THEY LISTENED

Read Jonah 3:1-10 from an easy-to-understand translation like the CEV, CEB, or a Bible storybook with pictures. You can also paraphrase the story. The following passage is from the CEV. As you read, consider pausing at various places and asking the children if they can imagine what is happening.

Once again the LORD told Jonah to go to that great city of Nineveh and preach his message of doom. Jonah obeyed the LORD and went to Nineveh. The city was so big that it took three days just to walk through it. After walking for a day, Jonah warned the people, "Forty days from now, Nineveh will be destroyed!" They believed God's message and set a time when they would go without eating to show their sorrow. Then everyone in the city, no matter who they were, dressed in sackcloth. When the king of Nineveh heard what was happening, he also dressed in sackcloth; he left the royal palace and sat in dust. Then he and his officials sent out an order for everyone in the city to obey. It said: None of you or your animals may eat or drink a thing. Each of you must wear sackcloth, and you must even put sackcloth on your animals. You must also pray to the LORD God with all your heart and stop being sinful and cruel. Maybe God will change his mind and have mercy on us, so we won't be destroyed. When God saw that the people had stopped doing evil things, he had pity and did not destroy them as he had planned.

Tell the group that this time when God tells Jonah to get up and go to Nineveh, Jonah goes. But he still isn't happy about it. The Bible tells us that Nineveh was such a big city that it would take three days to walk across it. Instead of walking to the middle of the city, which would take one and a half days, Jonah only walks for one day. Then he stops and tells the people that in forty days, God will destroy Nineveh. Jonah's message to Nineveh is only five words in the Hebrew language, and he doesn't give the people any hope. He just tells them that in forty days God will destroy the city. He shares as little as possible with them.

RESPONDING: GOD CAN USE ANYONE

Help the children understand the story by asking questions like these.

• Why do you think Jonah only told the people those five words? What else could he have told them?
• Have you ever done just enough to get by? If so, can you tell us about those times? (For example, a parent asks a child to clean his room and he puts everything under the bed. Or a parent asks a child to apologize to his sister and he mumbles, "I'm sorry" though he doesn't truly mean it.)
• What did the people of Nineveh do after Jonah talked to them? Does it surprise you that God was able to use Jonah to help these people even when Jonah didn't want to?

Explain that Jonah didn't want God to forgive the people, so he didn't tell them that God might forgive them. Somehow, the people still knew what to do. When they heard what Jonah said, they realized that they had done many wrong things, and they were sorry for what they had done. They believed what Jonah said and they repented. Jonah didn't want God to forgive the people, but God forgave Jonah when he ran from God. God forgave him. And when the people of Nineveh did wrong and then repented, God forgave them too.

This story reminds us that God uses people who make mistakes. Jonah wasn't perfect, but God used him to tell the people what would happen. Sometimes God does things we don't expect. In fact, God may use you to tell an adult about Jesus or to show an adult that he or she is wrong about someone else. God loves everyone and wants everyone to turn to God.

ALTERNATE OPTIONS: WHO CAN GOD SAVE?

For Preschoolers

Either print pictures of celebrities, teachers, parents, siblings, and other people in the children's lives, or simply read the following list, pausing after each name and asking if God can save that person no matter what he or she does.

- You
- Your mom
- Your dad
- Someone who lives in another country
- Your grandparents
- Your brother or sister
- A thief
- Your teacher
- Lunchroom worker at school
- A bully
- Your best friend
- Your neighbor
- Someone who has no home

Affirm the children's responses, correcting as needed, and then assure them that God can save everyone. God wants to forgive and save all of us. Jonah learned this the hard way. He wanted God to destroy the Ninevites, but they asked God to forgive them and showed God that they were sorry. And God saved them. God made each person in the world and loves us all as children.

For Younger Children

Remind the group that many unexpected things happened in the book of Jonah. The people of Nineveh didn't expect a prophet from God to come and talk to them. Jonah, the prophet, didn't expect God to forgive the Ninevites. The Ninevites didn't know God, but they obeyed immediately. Jonah, who loved God, did not obey at first. God does surprising things in our world too. Sometimes God uses someone we don't expect to teach us more about God. Ask questions like these: Who is someone you wouldn't expect to tell you about

God? Who might be surprised if you talked to them about God? Has God done something in your life that surprised you?

For Older Children
Before the Session: Prepare materials for the activity: paper, pencils/pens, trashcan, CD player with worship music.
Assure the children that all of us do things that are wrong sometimes. The Ninevites were doing a lot of things wrong, so God sent Jonah to tell them what would happen if they didn't repent. God was going to destroy the city, but the people realized that they were sinning. They felt sorry for the things they had done wrong. Instead of punishing them, God forgave them.

God forgives us too. In Romans 6, Paul says that sin brings death. God is perfect and we are not, so before Jesus came, there wasn't a way to be close to God. Then Jesus took all our sins away and died for us so that we can always be with God. God sent Jonah to tell the people to repent. Jonah told them a little about God. But when God sent Jesus, Jesus showed all people what it means to ask God to forgive us. And then Jesus did something even better: he forgave all of us, even the people who put him on the cross.

Like the Ninevites, sometimes we need to repent. Give each child some paper and a pencil or pen. As you play quiet worship music in the background, encourage them to write down some of the things they've done wrong. Ask them to say a silent prayer over the list, asking God to forgive them. Then guide them to tear up the paper over the trashcan and throw it all away. Tell them that the Bible says God throws our sins as far away as they can get. God has forgiven our sins, and we always have a new chance to start over.

SNACK TIME

Before the Session: Prepare something sweet to eat (cookies, cupcakes, etc.), and bring napkins and cups.
Give each child a sweet snack. Tell them that today we are eating something sweet to remind us that the people of Nineveh repented. When we repent, or tell God that we are sorry for our sins, God always forgives us. God also forgave the people of Nineveh and did not destroy their home. We eat something sweet because forgiveness is sweet! Say a prayer of thanksgiving together before you enjoy the snack.

MEMORY VERSE ACTIVITY

Memory Verse: "And the people of Nineveh believed God." (Jonah 3:5a)

Option 1

Let the group play the game "Hangman" on a white board or chalkboard to try to fill in the letters of the memory verse. Look online for simple directions to this common game.

Option 2

Before the Session: Write each word of the memory verse (including the reference) on eight separate index cards. Also bring masking tape.

Tape a prepared index card on each child's back. If your group is larger than eight children, tell those without index cards to put the ones with cards in order without talking. If you have eight children or less, have them work together to put themselves in order without talking. When they finish, read the memory verse out loud and have them practice saying it a few times.

Closing Prayer

God, thank you for forgiving all of us, even the people we may not like. Please help us look at others the way you see them: as your children just like we are. Amen.

YOU FORGAVE THEM?

Jonah 4:1-11

BEFORE THE SESSION

Read through the activities. Gather and/or prepare materials for the ones you choose. Become familiar with the Bible story.

WELCOME

Greet children with a smile and a welcome as they come into your classroom. Make sure they know that you're happy to be there with them!

OPENING ACTIVITY: PLANT A FLOWER

Before the Session: Gather the materials needed for children to plant their own flowers: plastic cups or small pots, soil, flower seeds, pitcher of water, plastic spoons, permanent marker to write names on cups or pots.

Tell the children that in today's story, a plant grows next to Jonah and gives him shade from the hot sun. Plants fill many of our needs: oxygen to breathe, food to eat, shade, and even medicine. Today the group will plant their own flowers to take home.

Give each child a cup or pot and a flower seed. Guide them to use a spoon to fill it halfway with potting soil. Then they should place a seed in the soil and cover it with more soil. As they work, ask if anyone knows what a plant needs to grow (soil, water, and sunlight). Help them water their planted seeds and tell them to find a sunny spot at home where the plant can grow. Remind them to be patient as they care for their plants and wait for them to sprout.

Say that in our story today, something strange happens to the plant that grew next to Jonah.

THE BIBLE STORY: YOU FORGAVE THEM?

Read Jonah 4:1-11 from an easy-to-understand translation like the CEV, CEB, or a Bible storybook with pictures. You can also paraphrase the story. The following passage is from the CEV. As you read, consider pausing at various places and asking the children if they can imagine what is happening. Remind them that Jonah is mad because when he told Nineveh that God would destroy their city, they repented and turned back to God.

Jonah was really upset and angry. So he prayed: "Our LORD, I knew from the very beginning that you wouldn't destroy Nineveh. That's why I left my own country and headed for Spain. You are a kind and merciful God, and you are very patient. You always show love, and you don't like to punish anyone, not even foreigners. Now let me die! I'd be better off dead." The LORD replied, "What right do you have to be angry?" Jonah then left through the east gate of the city and made a shelter to protect himself from the sun. He sat under the shelter, waiting to see what would happen to Nineveh. The LORD made a vine grow up to shade Jonah's head and protect him from the sun. Jonah was very happy to have the vine, but early the next morning the LORD sent a worm to chew on the vine, and the vine dried up. During the day the LORD sent a scorching wind, and the sun beat down on Jonah's head, making him feel faint. Jonah was ready to die, and he shouted, "I wish I were dead!" But the LORD asked, "Jonah, do you have the right to be angry about the vine?" "Yes, I do," he answered, "and I'm angry enough to die." But the Lord said: "You are concerned about a vine that you did not plant or take care of, a vine that grew up in one night and died the next. In that city of Nineveh there are more than a hundred twenty thousand people who cannot tell right from wrong, and many cattle are also there. Don't you think I should be concerned about that big city?

Tell the group that Jonah thought it was wrong for God to forgive the Ninevites because they were so bad. He had told the people that God would destroy them in forty days, but they were sorry for what they had done and began to worship God. God forgave them! Today we see how Jonah feels about God's mercy on the people of Nineveh.

RESPONDING: THE MERCY OF GOD

Help the children think about the story by asking questions like these:

• How did Jonah feel when God forgave the Ninevites?
• Why do you think Jonah went to sit on the hill? (Explain that he was waiting to see if God's mind would change.)
• Can you imagine trying to convince God *not* to forgive someone?
• Has it ever been hard for you to forgive someone who hurt you or people you love?

Talk about how it can be difficult to forgive people. Sometimes people do terrible things that deeply hurt us. Other times people say mean things that hurt us too. We don't know if the people of Nineveh did something to Jonah. All we know is that he didn't like them, and he wanted God to go ahead and destroy them. Did they deserve to be destroyed? Maybe. They had done a lot of bad things. But when they heard what was going to happen, they showed that they were sorry. They put on special clothing called sackcloth and fasted (did not eat) to show God how sorry they were. But that wasn't enough for Jonah. He still wanted them to be punished. God had to use a plant to remind Jonah to have compassion for other people, no matter how wrong they were.

ALTERNATE OPTIONS

Before the Session: Gather necessary supplies: paper, pencils, markers, and crayons.
For Preschoolers
Talk about what it means to forgive someone: they may hurt us in some way, but when they say they're sorry we are able to say, "That's okay. Thank you for apologizing." Tell the kids that it can be hard to forgive someone who makes us upset. Provide markers, crayons, and paper. Ask the children to draw a picture of a time when someone made them feel mad or sad.

Invite them to share their drawings if they wish, and then talk together about what happened in the situation they drew. Did the person say they were sorry? Were you able to forgive them? Assure the children that God loves us and always forgives us when we say we're sorry. God wants us to forgive people too.

For School-aged Children

Remind the children of last week's conversation about sins—the wrong things we do that may hurt others or ourselves. (The older kids made a list of sins, then tore it up and threw it in the trash to show that they were sorry and God forgave them.) Just like God forgave the Ninevites, God forgives us.

Admit that it can be hard for us to forgive people. Maybe someone has done something that hurt our feelings, or we did something that hurt ourselves or someone else. (If you like, share an age-appropriate story about something someone did when you were a child that hurt you and was hard to forgive. This is my story: When I was in elementary school, I had two best friends at school. We were like the three musketeers. But one day they decided they didn't want to be my friend anymore. They stopped talking to me and were mean to me when I tried to talk to them. It was hard to forgive them because I was hurt. But eventually, I was able to forgive them and let it go.)

Provide markers, crayons, and paper. Ask each child to write about something that happened that they need to forgive. They can write the first name of the other person involved if they wish. After a few minutes, pray together, asking God to help us forgive these people. Then guide the children to tear up the papers and throw them away to show that they have forgiven the people who upset or hurt them.

Note: Be sensitive to children in your group who have experienced situations involving alcohol, drugs, abuse, divorce, etc. Children should never be pressured to forgive people who have hurt them in this way, as that is a process that can take years. Such circumstances require professional assistance. If you know of or suspect something like this, talk to your pastor or a counselor for advice.

SNACK TIME

Before the Session: Prepare two different snack options: (1) something sour like sliced lemons, limes, oranges, or sour candies and (2) something sweet like strawberries, red apple slices, grapes, or donut holes. Bring cups for water.

Tell the group that Jonah had a sour attitude about the Ninevites; he didn't like them and he didn't want God to forgive them for the wrong things they did. But God always forgives those who repent, and this is a sweet truth! Today for snack, we have something sour and something sweet. Give the children the two snacks and talk about how each one tastes.

MEMORY VERSE ACTIVITY

Memory Verse: "You are a kind and merciful God, and you are very patient. You always show love . . . ." (from Jonah 4:2)

Write the memory verse and the reference on a white board or chalkboard. Depending on the size of your group, either assign each child one word (or the reference), or divide your class into small groups and assign each group a phrase from the verse. Have them shout out their words/phrases in the correct order. Next, have them stand in line in the correct order and shout out their words/phrases again.

Do this several times until the verse becomes familiar. Finally, have the entire group say the verse together.

CLOSING PRAYER

God, thank you for always forgiving us. Please help us forgive others and help us have a good attitude when we forgive. Amen.

Made in the USA
Lexington, KY
14 February 2019